The World Champion's Princess

The World Champion's Princess

Unbound & Unbroken

No more secrets

A family saga about

love, fear and betrayal

Dagmar Eckel

Address
Dagmar Eckel
Unterstr. 24
67745 Grumbach

Cover design: Claudia Sperl
Typesetting: Katja Zimiak
Writing support: Gerhard Mertin
Editing/proofreading: Natalie Dechant
Book marketing: Heike Paschke

ISBN E-book: 978-3-9827793-5-5
ISBN paperback: 978-3-9827793-3-1
ISBN hardcover: 978-3-9827793-4-8

Bibliographic information from the German National Library:
The German National Library lists this publication in the German National Bibliography; detailed bibliographic data is available on the Internet at http://dnb.d-nb.de.

Dedication

I dedicate this book to my parents, Horst and Hannelore Eckel, with deep gratitude and love. They were and remain my role models, because they always inspired me and gave me stability in my life. My mother was my father's great love, and their bond was so strong that it endured all the ups and downs of life. Their love lasted a lifetime.

Three years after my father's passing, I also had to say goodbye to my mother. But the love that united my parents lives on in my memory. Their lifelong song was 'Red Roses,' which accompanied them through the years and on every wedding anniversary, my father would give my mother a bouquet of her favorite flowers: roses. Each year, the bouquet would have one rose more than the previous year.

With love,
Your daughter,
Dagmar

Table of Contents

Foreword

With this book, I will take you on a journey, my journey, which is not only about glamour and fame. It is the story of the daughter of a 1954 World Cup champion. I did not always live in the public eye, but also lived in the shadow of my own story. I will open the doors to my life and let you take a look deep into my soul. You will learn about the good times, but also the difficult moments that have made me the person I am today. This book is honest, blunt, and provocative, because I want it to make you think.

I will give you deep insights into my family history, into stories that will make you laugh, think, and (perhaps) cry. You will see that my life was anything but a fairy tale. Many people think that I always stood in my father's light, but there were just as many moments when I had to act in the background, when the glory did not belong to me, and when I had to step into the shadows myself to protect my father. Everything in life has its price, even the spotlight. I paid that price a long time ago. But it was precisely these experiences that shaped me and led me to dedicate myself to preserving the legacy of my father and Germany's 1954 World Cup soccer team.

Often, only the glamour and the positive aspects are seen, and those certainly existed. I won't deny that. But what about the shadows that fame brings with it? What about the stories that are never told?

I have carried my father's legacy throughout my life, not only the glorious moments, but also the difficult ones. Yes, I always stayed close to my father, not for self-promotion, but out of a sense of responsibility. I had felt this responsibility even as a child, and as my father grew older, it became stronger and stronger. I had to protect him when the public became too much for him. And now that he is no longer here, I also carry on the responsibility for his legacy.

I feel a deep responsibility to continue this legacy through the Horst Eckel Foundation, yet this is not a task I can manage in isolation. I must put my face and name forward publicly to generate support, as the Heroes of Bern can no longer fight this battle themselves. They require our collective assistance. My approach is always one of unwavering authenticity, even when that is polarizing and makes me a thorn in the side of some. I've learned I can't satisfy every person; my ultimate goal is to satisfy myself, so I can remain true to my purpose.

I invite you to join me in reflection, to smile, and to react and raise the difficult questions, for my efforts alone are not enough. It is only in our unity that we can ensure the myth of 1954 endures, and that its legacy is passed down to future generations.

Dagmar Eckel

A Final Token of Love

I sat down at my father's desk, which was a mess of memories: photos, newspaper clippings, legal documents, papers concerning our house, videotapes, and a clutter of letters. The correspondence ranged from friends and acquaintances to fan mail—autograph requests that still arrive even today. But nestled among them were the love letters my father had written to my mother. It was these letters that showed me a man completely different from the public figure everyone thought they knew.

To the public, my father, Horst Eckel, was known as the famous soccer player, "the greyhound," a nickname he earned due to his incredible running ability. He was also a member of the "Heroes of Bern," the legendary team that achieved a sensational and completely unexpected World Cup victory in 1954.

My eyes scanned the familiar awards, medals, certificates, and trophies adorning the room, pulling my thoughts back to the early morning of Friday, December 3rd, just a few days prior. I had barely slept, but perhaps I drifted off briefly, because I awoke to find several missed calls on my phone from the hospital in Landstuhl where my father was a patient.

That morning remains vivid in my memory. A rush of thoughts consumed me as I drove to Landstuhl. I recall taking the elevator to his ward, hurrying down the long corridor, where the attending physician greeted me with a somber expression. Patients stood whispering quietly, casting furtive glances my way. In that moment, I understood they already knew: my father had died earlier that morning. A chilling fear also gripped me—that the news had spread beyond the hospital walls. Soon, calls started coming in from acquaintances that confirmed this fear. The news had broken before I could even release it to the press myself.

As the last surviving member of the 1954 World Cup-winning team, my father's passing was bound to elicit a public response. The varying nature of these reactions became clear to me the very next night.

The night after his death, around 3 AM, a call came in about a break-in at Horst Eckel's house. The thieves were presumably after valuables that had taken on special significance after his passing. I remember the incident vividly; my heart pounded, and my thoughts raced. I was deeply shocked, immediately thinking of my mother, who still lived in my parents' house with her caregiver.

Fortunately, the news of the break-in was only partially accurate. There had indeed been an attempted break-in, but not at my parents' house. Instead, it was at the Horst Eckel House in Kusel, the old school building where my father used to teach. Nevertheless, the mere idea that someone would break into the Horst Eckel House while we were still mourning my father was unbearable. It felt as if they were trying to erase not only him but also the very traces of his life.

This incident highlighted the immediate necessity of securing my father's valuable possessions, including the awards he had earned throughout his sporting and social life. A lawyer friend advised me that I was responsible for these items and needed to ensure their safe keeping.

Preserving the memories

I knew I had to act. I had to preserve his memories, for myself, for my family, for everyone who had accompanied him on his journey. The battle for the honorary grave was arduous, full of red tape. But in the end, it was worth it. Now he rests there, together with my mother and my grandparents, in a place worthy of him. But when, after two years, I finally had the gravestone I had designed with love and care erected, it was defaced—with dirt, with toothpaste. To this day, I don't know who did it or why. Was it hatred? Envy? Disrespect? I'll probably never know.

But what I do know is that it was a blow to the heart. And yet I knew I wouldn't let it break me.

Then a letter arrived. A "condolence letter" that accused me of killing my father through insufficient care. I'd spent my life learning to cope with hostility, insults, and anonymous attacks. But this was different—it wasn't just hurtful; it was inhumane. Still, I resolved not to let it consume me. I will fight back, for my parents and for my father, who taught me: "Human dignity is inviolable. Never elevate yourself above others."

In addition to the grief of loss, I now had to worry about my father's legacy, these visible traces of his life. All the certificates and trophies were as familiar to me as if they were my own, some more so than others: the gold medal for winning the 1954 World Cup, a refrigerator that each of the national players at the time had received, the medals for the two German championships that my father had won with his club, 1. FC Kaiserslautern, his jerseys worn during important games, the countless photos of him with his teammates from Kaiserslautern, Werner Liebrich, Werner Kohlmayer, Ottmar Walter, and of course Fritz Walter, who was like a father figure to the young Horst Eckel, the signed photos from his career in the national team. For decades, I saw most of them almost every day. They were part of our house like the furniture, including the massive, old German desk at which I now sat. But of course, these things were not my property; they belonged to my father (and now to my mother), and he had cherished them throughout his life.

In the days that followed, I tried to sort through and organize everything, but I found it increasingly difficult because, although I knew almost every piece, I didn't know the background of each one. I remembered that I had wanted to ask my father about a particular piece from time to time. But my mother often blocked my questions and withheld some things. Today, I ask myself why I wasn't more persistent, why I didn't ask more questions. Now I will never be able to ask them, and this finality is difficult for me to bear. During this time, I often had the feeling that my father might suddenly come into the room and say, "Why didn't you ask me earlier?"

In those moments, I felt incredibly close to him. Sometimes I would discover something somewhere in our house that I hadn't seen in a long time, and I had the feeling that he had deliberately led me to that spot. But there are some places he hasn't led me to yet. I am still looking for the jersey he brought back from the 1958 World Cup, his second and last one. Unfortunately, this jersey hasn't been found, but there is a document that proves that it was in our possession.

The jersey, like hundreds of other items, was part of our family's collection, belonging to my father. Now, the responsibility fell to me to protect them from damage or loss. However, I soon realized that even with the best intentions, this task would prove challenging.

I received the most criticism for auctioning off some of my father's possessions. People only saw that memorabilia was being sold, but they didn't understand why. They didn't know the full story—I do. I know that I did it out of love for my mother. My father and mother had worked tirelessly their entire lives. They weren't millionaires, as so many people assumed. They had to work hard for everything they achieved, with dedication, discipline, and always prioritizing family. I had promised my mother that I would never place her in a nursing home—that I would care for her and make her final years as comfortable and pleasant as possible. And that is precisely what I did, no doubt about it. I set high standards for myself, and I met them.

After my father passed away, it was up to me to tell my mother that we needed to make some changes. I explained to her that it was essential to ensure she lived the life she deserved. It broke my heart a little, but she was strong, always strong. She lived for another three years, and while I didn't know how much time she had left, I was determined to do everything I could to give her that time. Despite all my father's careful planning, it was clear that the money would eventually run out. With the partial auction I created a financial buffer that allowed her to continue living the life she had always wanted. I made that happen for her. No one has the right to judge that.

When strength is no longer enough

The months leading up to my father's death were busy and, at times, very hectic. His 90th birthday was approaching, and preparations for the celebrations were in full swing. After all, my father was the last surviving member of the "legendary" German national team that won the World Cup in Switzerland in 1954. That victory gave the German people a renewed sense of self-worth at a time when they felt like the losers and the guilty party after World War II..

Sadly, he didn't live to see his 90th birthday on February 8, 2022. The strength and tenacious will that had defined him as a soccer player simply weren't enough anymore. Two severe accidents at home had significantly weakened him. It was too much, as we, his family, realized. On December 3, 2021, he passed away peacefully, and we accepted it, understanding it was what he had wished.

My father's death didn't happen suddenly. It arrived quietly, like a long-anticipated guest with their coat in hand, yet still lingering. The day after he passed, I sat at my desk—a sturdy, dark wood piece of furniture that had absorbed so many stories, I sometimes imagined it would begin recounting them itself through its fine scratches, rough surface, and the grooves from my nervous finger drumming.

Old letters, yellowed photos, and documents lay before me. Some of the pictures had faded, others were sharp and full of life, yet they all suddenly seemed unreal. It was as if they no longer belonged in my life but in a closed chapter I was now opening with trembling fingers. Downstairs in the living room sat my mother; the nurse was in the kitchen. I heard the sounds—quiet footsteps, running water, the clattering of dishes. No voices. No music. Just this silence, which wasn't empty, but heavy. I knew I should go to her. A few words, a touch. But I couldn't yet. First, I had to face my own inner chaos and the man who had been my father.

I pulled out an old notebook. It smelled of leather and the past. When I opened it, I recognized his clear, careful, and disciplined handwriting.

No grand confessions. Just lists, addresses, and little notes. Yet, I read more than just words in it. I read him. His essence. His sense of order. His modesty. "What now?" I whispered, stroking the paper as if I could feel his hand on it. There was no answer, only silence. I began to organize photos by year, letters by importance, documents in labeled envelopes. Not because I had to, but because it gave me stability—an action amidst speechlessness, an attempt to hold on to what was threatening to dissolve: his life, his dignity, his legacy, and the protection of my mother.

I remembered a conversation we'd had long before his death. It wasn't one of those deep, meaningful talks, but rather a casual moment, the kind that sometimes happens between a father and daughter—unassuming yet unforgettable. "When I'm gone… you'll know what to do," he had said. At the time, I remained silent. Now I knew: I would do it. Out of love. For him. For her. For us.

I pulled a photo from the stack. My father, young, with that mischievous smile I had so often looked for in my own face. Beside him, my mother, beautiful, lively, and radiant. They stood in front of a stadium, laughing as if the world were their playground. I blinked away tears. "Not now," I murmured, thinking of the call I'd received two days earlier. Of the calm, matter-of-fact voice on the other end. "I'm sorry…" Then: silence. And then the moment I had to tell my mother. She was silent. She didn't cry. But her gaze said it all: "He would have wanted us to be strong." Strong. What did that even mean? I felt anything but strong, yet I felt responsible. For her. For him. For what remains when a person leaves. I took a deep breath and reached for the next envelope. My hands stopped shaking. I was ready.

The 84th Minute—A Life Dedicated to Sport

A few days after going through my father's belongings in Vogelbach, I found some time at home to look through the newspaper articles reporting his death. I noticed that they repeatedly emphasized that my father, at 22, was the youngest player on the legendary team that played in the 1954 World Cup final and, until recently, was the last of them still alive. It was also often mentioned that Hungary had been considered the odds-on favorite by experts. "The predictions of the soccer experts seemed to be confirmed after just eight minutes, as Hungary quickly took a 2-0 lead," most newspaper reports about the final began. "But the German team quickly scored their first goal and managed to tie the game before the end of the first half. In the second half, the game was evenly balanced, and neither team managed to score another goal at first."

As I read these lines, I immediately thought of the book my father had written in 2004 to mark the 50th anniversary of Germany's World Cup victory, together with author Volker Neumann, entitled "Die 84. Minute" (The 84th Minute). In it, he describes the decisive moments of the final as follows:

"I'm positioned 40, maybe 42 meters in front of the Hungarian penalty area, slightly to the right—that's my spot. The rain is absolutely pouring down. Hans (Schäfer) is on the left side, battling for the ball with Bozsik. The Boss (Helmut Rahn) is moving 20 meters ahead of me, heading toward the Hungarian box. My opponent, Hidegkuti, runs past me into the Hungarian half, right into my line of sight. Despite that, I can see that Hans has stolen the brown leather ball from Bozsik and is dribbling a few more steps. 'In!' shouts Ottmar Walter, who is also sprinting toward the Hungarian penalty area. I notice Max Morlock is practically standing on the penalty spot. I see the ball fly into the Hungarian box as a high cross, somehow catch a glimpse of Ottmar, and then see a Hungarian defender—I can't tell if it's Lantos or Zakarias—clear the ball out of the box. 'Cleared,' I think, and I'm just starting to brace myself for the inevitable Hungarian counter-attack. I look for Hidegkuti, but suddenly I see the cleared ball flying directly into Helmut Rahn's path; I watch The Boss control it. I start moving forward again, two or three meters, toward the center, leaving my position, almost halfway to the left, both hands on my hips. In that split second, I realize: The Boss isn't going to pass; he's going to shoot."

"Helmut shifts the ball from his right foot to his left, getting past the player rushing him—I think it's Zakarias. Hidegkuti crosses my line of sight again, forcing me to lean slightly to the left just as the ball hits the post in the bottom right corner of the Hungarian goal."

"A fraction of a second passes. Grosics, the Hungarian goalkeeper, is still on the ground when the cheers from tens of thousands of our fans erupt in a deafening roar."

I have read this passage in my father's book countless times and know it almost by heart. Nevertheless, it always makes me feel a bit euphoric when I pick up the book again, as I just have done now.

The press often called our win against the heavy favorite, Hungary, a sensation. But for my father, it was nothing of the sort. "We were a close, tight-knit group where everyone fought for each other," he always stressed. "That was a major factor in our success. We knew we were strong enough to beat Hungary. We had a great team."

My father always viewed his sport as a close-knit community—a team effort. This is evident in his book, "Die 84. Minute" (The 84th Minute), where he recounts how Richard Schneider, the coach of his home club, 1. FC Kaiserslautern, suddenly wanted to move him from the forward to a defensive position two years before the World Cup in Switzerland. As he wrote in his book, my father wasn't thrilled about having to become a defensive player when he was clearly an attacker. However, he went along with it, only to conclude: "And to my own surprise, it worked quite well. The way I played with Werner Liebrich and Fritz Walter felt like we'd been doing it that way all along."

He later discovered that the strategy originated with the national coach at the time, Sepp Herberger, who had been fine-tuning his team for two years before the World Cup. My father, the former forward—nicknamed "the Greyhound" for his stamina and speed—accepted his role. In the final in Bern, he was able to "neutralize Nandor Hidegkuti, the brilliant playmaker of the Hungarian attack," as one newspaper reported after the match. "Horst Eckel executed this with a consistency that can rightly be considered the key to victory."

Dr. Friedebert Becker, who covered the 1954 World Cup for soccer newspaper "Kicker" and was one of the most respected soccer reporters of the era, described Eckel's performance in almost dramatic terms: "Horst Eckel's fluid technique was key to his numerous successes against the clever, unpredictable Hidegkuti. Only twice did his intense focus cause him to push too far forward on the attack. His dynamic with Werner Liebrich and Fritz Walter was brilliant. Eckel was a powerful anchor for the 'invisible' Kaiserslautern defensive line, protecting the German goal. He positioned himself intelligently for passes and wisely avoided unnecessary dribbling. It was the most seasoned performance yet from the young player out of Kaiserslautern.'

Even though my father never liked the term, he and his teammates were henceforth referred to as the "Heroes of Bern." "We are not heroes," he always said, "we are just normal people."

Horst and Hannelore: A Love That Never Ended

It was the moment that would forever shape my father's life, even though he had no idea at the time how deeply it would impact his future. My father was eight years old when he visited his older friend, my uncle Werner. Werner was seven years older than my father and twelve years older than my mother. It was in this unexpected moment that fate showed itself.

In the courtyard, where the children were playing happily, they came to the sandbox. My mother, then only three years old, was sitting there completely absorbed in her own little world. She was a lively child—sweet as sugar, with dark, shiny curls, big brown eyes, and a small, cheeky snub nose. Even back then, she had the charm of a girl who stood out for her intelligence and alert mind. But at that age it wasn't her charm that won hearts—at least not my father's. To him and Uncle Werner, she was just a little girl playing in the sandbox, enthusiastically building sandcastles and not interested in the bigger boys

My father, who was very determined, looked at her for a while. Then he said, as if it was the most normal thing in the world, and with a smile that reflected his determination: "Hey, Werner, I want to marry your sister." A sentence that didn't impress anyone at the time, because my mother paid no attention to the two of them. The sandbox was her world, and nothing could disturb her concentration as she built. But as in all the best stories, that would later change.

The years passed. The little princess covered in sand grew into a young woman. And the cheeky boy grew into a young man who won her heart in ways he himself would never have thought possible. Their relationship was passionate, with ups and downs. They loved each other, they argued, they reconciled, and they always found their way back to each other. Sometimes they argued so loudly that the neighbors shook their heads. But no one doubted that they belonged together.

Lake Constance became an important place to them. They shared many beautiful and turbulent moments there. It was the place where my father threw her pants into the water during an argument and later laughed as he apologized. It was where they celebrated their engagement on a balmy summer evening. And it was the place they returned to for their first vacations together, far away from everyday life, with the many dreams they shared.

Then came the day of their wedding. It wasn't a big celebration, there was no fuss, but it was marked by their deep love and the promise to share a life together, come what may. And they kept their promise.

Many years later, my father fell ill and ended up in hospital. My mother was by his side. She did not leave his side, she held his hand, encouraged him and supported him through this difficult time. When he died, she was with him all the way, showing the same love and determination that she had as a little girl in the sandbox. She lived for three more years, but during that time he was always there. In her thoughts and in her heart, he was always with her.

So their story ends as it began—with a little girl in the sandbox and a boy who already knew back then that she was his future.

Always by His Side in the Hospital

On September 12, 1954, at the local derby between soccer clubs 1. FC Kaiserslautern and VfR Kaiserslautern, my father suffered a serious fracture to his tibia and fibula. The injury was a bitter setback for him, for his club FCK, and also for the national team. He had to take a break for almost a whole year. For someone like my father, who was an athlete through and through, this was almost unbearable. Suddenly, he was no longer on the soccer field, but lying still in a hospital bed in Kaiserslautern. The days were long and the pain severe.

His teammates Ottmar Walter, Werner Liebrich, Fritz Walter, and Kohlmeier would visit him. They wanted to cheer him up, distract him a little, show him that he hadn't been forgotten. But apart from these brief visits, he had very little contact with the outside world. Even his own mother was advised not to come so that he could fully concentrate on his recovery.

Only one person was allowed to see him regularly, my mother. She was seventeen years old at the time. Although she was officially "just" his girlfriend, her place was by his side. She was not deterred by anything, not by rules, not by conventions. Her love was silent, strong, and unwavering. To keep the press from getting wind of this, the hospital staff secretly let her in through the back entrance. They weren't really happy about it; they only wanted to allow it once. But when the nurses and doctors noticed how my father perked up when she was with him, how he laughed, how his mood improved, how even the healing process was visibly accelerated, they simply let her be.

From then on, she was allowed to come whenever she wanted. And she came every day. She held his hand, encouraged him, and was there for him—quiet, determined, full of love. What could have been a dark, painful time became, thanks to her closeness, a warm, almost luminous chapter in his memory and in our family story. On August 21, 1955, almost a year later, my father was back on the soccer field. He made his comeback in an international match against the Soviet Union in Moscow. But the real new beginning did not start there, it began in a hospital room in Kaiserslautern, where a young girl with a clear vision and a strong heart had brought him back to life. He told me this again and again from when I was a child, in his own voice.

When My Father Talks About Love and Happiness

It wasn't always easy, but it was always real. Even when I first saw her, the girl with the braids, who always stood a little to the side, her head held high, and who never laughed out loud with the others, I knew she was special. Hannelore. I had had my eye on her for a long time, back when we used to go to the woods with our group of friends, dancing and laughing, and I secretly played my accordion so I could be part of the fun. But even though we belonged together, it was never entirely clear whether she felt the same way I did. I was too shy to just tell her or ask her.

After the 1954 final, when we were celebrated as world champions, I sat in Berlin, in the middle of the crowd, music was playing, the cheering was deafening, but there was only one thought in my head: When I get home, I'll finally be able to dance with Hannelore. I will show her that I am not just the guy who is always playing music or soccer, but also the one who wants to see her dance, who wants to feel her closeness.

Then came the day when I arrived back in Vogelbach after the world championship title. The car stopped in front of our gate, and I was brought out from under a blanket so that no one would see me, but just like in a big city, people stood in rows, bicycles, motorcycles, and cars lined up like in the Pied Piper of Hamelin. The band was playing, my mother and sister were standing in front of the house, and everyone was shouting my name. But one person held back: Hannelore. A friend of hers came to the car. I asked: "Where is Hanne?" She gestured to the right. There she stood, her head held high with pride, her braids still the same as before, her face calm, but her eyes shining. She held a flower bouquet intended for me, but did not bring it to the car herself. She didn't want to be the center of attention. She didn't want me to see her the way everyone else saw me that day. And this bouquet—this small, quiet bouquet from her—was the most beautiful gift I have ever received.

I loved her since I first set eyes on her. But it wasn't so easy to show her my love. I remember exactly how I went to the GUM department store in Moscow in 1955 to buy her a small bottle of perfume. That was almost unaffordable for me at the time. I walked back and forth through the perfume department several times, the scents wafted around my nose, and my teammates grinned from afar because they knew exactly who the bottle was for. Finally, I decided on a small, light blue bottle of Russian perfume, which I then carefully carried in my hand luggage for the entire journey home.

When I got home, I gave my mother caviar, my sister a tin—and Hannelore? I still had to find my opportunity. After several failed attempts, repeatedly interrupted because someone from our friends' group was always around, I finally spoke to her: "Hannelore, would you like to go to the movies with me on Sunday?" She smiled at me and said: "Yes, I'd love to." I felt like I was walking on cloud nine. Sunday came, the home game was over, I showered, got dressed, and set off on my scooter. But shortly before I arrived at Hannelore's house, I remembered: Oh no! I had forgotten the perfume! How could that have happened? It was still at home on the kitchen table. I rushed back; my sister had got curious and tried it out in the meantime, but luckily, she had hardly used any. I took the bottle, ran back, rang the bell—and there she stood in a fancy green summer dress, beaming.

At the cinema, while the film starring Curd Jürgens was playing, I feverishly tried to work out when I should give her the perfume. Finally, shortly before the film ended, I pulled the bottle out of my jacket pocket, leaned over to her, and whispered: "Hey, Hannelore, I brought you something back from Moscow." She smiled, took it, and said quietly: "Thank you, that's very kind of you." From that moment on, it was clear that we were a couple. Our relationship grew more intense with each passing day. She was never particularly interested in soccer, but that wasn't important to me. She never saw me as the athlete, but always as the person, Horst. That was exactly what made us so special.

On Easter Sunday, 1957, we got engaged, and on November 25 of the same year, we married in the collegiate church in Kaiserslautern. It was a Monday because there was an away game on Sunday. Many of my teammates, even my coach Richard Schneider, and my friend Fritz Walter, my best man, were there. Shortly after the wedding, I moved into my parents-in-law's house, and later into my parents' house after it was renovated. Hannelore and I had two wonderful daughters. Susanne was born first, followed six years later by Dagmar.

Dagmar was very like me, she loved soccer as much as I did, and had the same values and sense of humor. From the very beginning, we were connected by an invisible bond. However, since I was away a lot, this bond only grew stronger when Dagmar was about seventeen years old. The series Riptide allowed us to re-establish a closer relationship. From then on, she accompanied me, often alongside my wife, until Hannelore was no longer able to travel.

She became my support and later also my protective shield. She took over my wife's role as my manager, my mouthpiece, my heart. I always said to her: “If not you, then who?” I knew that when I was no longer around, my legacy would be in the best hands with her.

That's my story. The story of a boy from Vogelbach who loved soccer, but loved Hannelore even more.

But it is also my story, without which I, Dagmar Eckel, would never have existed.

A Nocturnal Bath and an Almost Scandalous Way Home

It was a beautiful day on vacation at Lake Constance in the late 1950s, shortly after my parents' wedding. The sun was shining, the air was warm, and our mood couldn't have been better. My parents spent that evening partying with my aunt Ilse and my uncle Robert.

But as so often happens when things get too quiet, a minor argument broke out that day. It was just a misunderstanding, just a trifle. My mother had once again gotten upset over something trivial, my father lost his temper, and just like that, there was a big argument. Since both were extremely proud people, neither of them would give in.

"Fine, then I'll just go alone with Ilse and Robert," said my mother with a mixture of determination and defiance. "All right, then go!" my father replied, but deep down he already knew what he would do. He always had a mischievous twinkle in his eye, his blue eyes sparkling with anticipation for what he would do next. He would watch her, secretly follow her, and—as always—play one of his legendary pranks.

And so it was. The three of them boarded the boat and enjoyed a pleasant trip across Lake Constance. They sang, danced, drank champagne, and had a great time. My father, always close behind, watched the whole thing calmly. He was just waiting for the right moment to strike. His blue eyes sparkled with anticipation. He knew exactly where they were and what they were doing.

Afterwards, my mother would always say: "I have no idea how he did it. We didn't see him; there weren't many people on the boat." But my father always them in his sights. The evening passed, and finally my father seized his opportunity. The three decided to take a nighttime swim in Lake Constance. The mood was lively, the air was warm, and the water looked very tempting. However, they didn't have their bathing suits with them. So they spontaneously decided to swim naked.

But secretly, my mother also used this situation to teach my father a little lesson. She knew him well and was sure that if he found out about this, he would not be impressed.

Without hesitation, they placed their clothes under a tree, and with a collective "Oh, come on, what the heck, let's just go into the water!" they all jumped into the cool water.

At that time—the late 1950s—society was still very reserved and conservative. For many people, swimming naked was scandalous, especially if it didn't take place in a private setting. The idea of splashing around in the water in the middle of the night, in full view of the public and without clothes, was very daring and actually quite progressive for that time. It was almost a small act of rebellion against the prudish society in which they lived. And that was precisely what made the moment even more exciting—not just the swimming itself, but also the feeling of doing something that was still considered a little too "liberal" in the late 1950s.

What the three of them didn't know was that my father had been observing them for some time. From his point of view, my mother's swimming naked in Lake Constance, without him, and especially since Uncle Robert was there, was shocking. So he quietly slipped away from his observation post when they went into the water and devised an ingenious plan. He took all their clothes, gathered them up calmly, and climbed a tree. From up there, he had the perfect view of the spectacle that was about to take place.

Eventually, the fun was over, and the three swimmers waded out of the water, laughing. But as soon as they reached the shore, reality struck.

Silence.

Then horrified shouting: "Where are our clothes?!" My mother spun around frantically, aunt Ilse tripped over a root, and uncle Robert cursed quietly to himself. Everyone stared at the ground where their clothes should have been lying, but there was nothing there. They started to panic. They searched and searched, but their clothes had vanished without a trace.

"We left them HERE, didn't we?!"

"Maybe just over there?"

"I can't see anything—oh my God, oh my God, OH MY GOD!"

They felt their way through the grass, crawled almost on all fours, pushing branches aside. Meanwhile, my father was up the tree, trying to suppress his laughter. It was just too funny! He could no longer bear to watch the spectacle and decided it was time to reveal his clever ruse. Slowly, very slowly, he let the first items of clothing fall from the branches of the tree.

BAM—my mother reached out and grabbed a shirt.

Whoosh–aunt Ilse caught a towel.

PLOP–uncle Robert caught a hat.

A hat! No shirt, no pants, not even a decent towel, just a hat. My father could hardly contain his laughter. He turned the pieces of clothing in his hands, then slowly looked down and surveyed the scene below. Three naked people who were desperately trying to maintain some dignity with only a hat and a towel. The longest and probably most embarrassing walk ever through Nonnenhorn began. My mother, in a shirt that was much too big and kept coming undone, aunt Ilse, who wrapped the towel around herself so tightly it looked as if it was going to save her life, and uncle Robert—poor guy!—desperately trying to cover the barest minimum with a single hat. The hat was frantically turned from front to back, depending on who was coming towards them.

Of course, they met people along the way, how could it be otherwise? The first passerby cleared his throat and said, somewhat confused: "Um. .. good evening..." Another one murmured: "Nice... hat." "Lovely night, isn't it?" someone exclaimed when they saw them on the street.

On the way to the inn, an elderly gentleman commented dryly: "Well, that's what I call a swimming party." Finally, some degree of rescue was in sight, as my father secretly placed the clothes on a wall. He now felt a little sorry for the bathers. As if out of nowhere, my mother, aunt Ilse, and uncle Robert found the clothes when they passed by the wall. Without giving much thought to this strange coincidence, they hurriedly put on their clothes, each trying to preserve what little dignity they had left as they made their way back to the inn.

At last, they reached the inn. But my father hadn't just waited for them, he was already one step ahead. He sneaked into the inn ahead of them, disappeared into the room, and waited patiently for the three arrivals to eventually find him. He knew that they would have a story to tell him; of course, not without a certain feeling of triumph in the back of his mind.

There he was, sitting in his room, looking completely innocent and grinning widely, when they finally entered. At first, they couldn't help but tell the story with a mixture of shyness and anger. As they told their stories, it must have finally dawned on them that there had to be more to it than that. Especially this strange coincidence, that the clothes suddenly appeared on the wall as if by magic, gave them a moment of clarity. That was the moment when my father had to confess. Anyone who knew my mother's temper knows that it would have been extremely unpleasant for him to reveal his prank. He must have wished he was back in his tree at that moment.

I can imagine that my mother wasn't exactly jumping for joy when she told him about their desperate attempts to hide in bushes and behind walls, as she slowly realized who she had to thank for this whole ordeal. I would have loved to have been a fly on the wall. But as is often the case in our family, the whole thing quickly blew over. The story was told again and again, everyone would laugh, and eventually my mother and father found their smiles again and reconciled—with a wink and a shared giggle about the prank my father would recount again and again over the years.

Swimming Trunks at Lake Constance—A Love with a Strong Pull

After their wedding, my parents went on vacation to Lake Constance again. It was a wonderful morning, the sun was shining, the lake was glistening, and it was so warm that you literally wanted to jump straight in. My mother was not yet an experienced swimmer. She had only just learned to stay afloat and still felt a bit afraid in the deep water. Despite this—or perhaps because of it—she really wanted to get into the water. My father, on the other hand, was a more leisurely type. He had made himself comfortable on the beach towel and didn't even think about plunging into the cool water.

Of course, my mother didn't like that at all. She wanted him to come into the water with her, but because he refused, she stomped off with feigned determination. She walked down the jetty to the small ladder leading into the water and climbed down. My father didn't take his eyes off her for a second—ever the attentive husband, even as he tried to remain casually reclined on his towel. My mother swam a few laps to prove to him how safe she already felt. But at some point, she realized that she had overestimated her strength. The water became deeper, her arms heavy, her legs tired. With her last energy, she swam back to the ladder. But—oh no!—there was already another man there who was just about to climb up!

In her moment of greatest need, my mother reached for the only support available to her—which was, well, the man's swimming trunks. With the last of her strength, she clung tight and pulled. The poor man was completely taken by surprise. He hadn't noticed her at all and probably thought at first that the water was pulling at his trunks. He tried to hold on to the ladder while desperately pulling his trunks back up with one hand. But my mother, who was now half hanging on the swimming trunks, kept pulling on them courageously, and each time they slipped down a little further.

The poor man desperately tried to climb up, pulling up his trunks with one hand while the other clung desperately to the ladder. My mother, on the other hand—half laughing, half panicking—kept pulling on them as if her life depended on it (which, to her, it did). It was a wild back and forth. She pulled down, he pulled up, she pulled down again, he pulled up again—a real tug-of-war over the swimming trunks!

Meanwhile, my father sat on the beach towel, shaking his head and laughing, enjoying the spectacle. He knew that my mother wasn't really in danger, but the sight was just too funny. Hanne, he thought, always in the middle of the chaos. At some point, he, too, had had enough of the spectacle. He got up, went to the ladder, and first helped the poor man, whose swimming trunks were now hanging halfway down, and then my mother, who was still clinging to him for dear life. When she finally made it out, still out of breath and with that famous hint of defiance in her voice, she simply said: "I told you, you should have come with me!" My father just shrugged his shoulders with a grin and said: "Women! And especially mine."

Laugh, Love, and Live

It was a different time back then. A time when people still wrote letters to ask for parents' consent to marry, a time when love was not conveyed through screens and instant messages, but through genuine encounters, trust, and patient anticipation. It was 1957 when my parents got engaged—my mother just twenty years old, my father twenty-five. It was an engagement made shortly before his journey into the wide world, to the United States, a step taken with care and my grandparents' approval. My mother often told me with a twinkle in her eye how they went to the registry office with my grandparents' signatures. They had given their blessing because they loved my father as if he were their own son. For my father, they were not only parents-in-law, they were mother and father. They were his rock, teaching him what trust and family really mean.

Nevertheless, my mother often confessed to me that she had doubts at the beginning. Doubts as to whether this great love could really also become a life lived. Whether two such spirited people as she and my father could manage to truly understand each other. But love had won out.

Over time, she realized that my father was her great love. He became the center of her life, the rock on which she could lean and which also carried her through when life became stormy.

After their wedding, my mother often told me with a wink how they moved into their room in her parents' house—an old bed, huge down comforters that they almost sank into when they first jumped on them together. They laughed, loved, and lived life. Before the wedding, they had hardly been allowed to touch each other, but now they were finally free to start their life together. Nevertheless, when they were engaged and staying at Lake Constance—in separate hotels, as was customary at the time—their time together was full of little adventures. My father, who was already a well-known soccer player, would sneak into my mother's hotel secretly in the evenings. The people in Nonnenhorn gossiped, but never maliciously. It was a sweet story that only brought joy. This story remained within the family, in this place that always felt a little bit like home to us.

Years later, when I was about ten, I traveled to Nonnenhorn with my parents. I had just had an appendectomy, and I was still weak, but this time was like a gift because I had my parents all to myself. I remember having lunch alone with my father, where I was served trout Mullerin style, a delicacy he chose from the menu with a twinkle in his eye, as if he wanted to show me the world. As always, the rule was that the plate had to be cleaned. After all, I was taught that food is valuable and that you have to behave properly at the table. But on that day, under the blazing midday sun, amid conversations about soccer and life, something happened. The fish on my plate had apparently decided to consider the journey to my stomach merely a stopover, and so it sought its way back out into the wide world in a quick, determined arc.

Halfway over the bridge, I was overcome by a queasy feeling, the fish seemed to quietly say "bye bye!" and I threw up—not once, but four or five times. My father stood next to me, slightly overwhelmed, but with that mischievous grin I knew so well. "It wasn't me, I honestly didn't do anything!" he insisted later with a wink, as my mother put me to bed at home with a mixture of concern and amusement. I felt better the next day. This trip remains one of my most precious memories. I had my parents all to myself, without the public, without their obligations to others—just the three of us, laughing at the little runaway fish that wanted to see the world one more time.

My mother always told me my parents' wedding was like something out of a fairy tale. She wore a white dress, which she later cut shorter and wore again and again. "The princess has found her prince," people said. But it was not an easy love story. It was life with its ups and downs, its passionate discussions, loudly slammed doors, but also with the unshakeable love that endured through it all. My parents both had strong personalities, and especially when it came to us children, there were often clashes. But in the end, they always found their way back to each other. Their marriage was not a romanticized idyll, but rather the real, lived life that connected them—until my father died at the age of 89 and my mother followed him three years later. She always said that my father was her great love, and without him, she was incomplete.

I remember how much my father relied on my mother. She managed the family, kept things running smoothly, took care of the finances, organized everything, and handled all the smaller and bigger things in everyday life. When my father drove to the gas station or went out for a beer, she gave him the money he needed. We children always jokingly called it "Dad's allowance." But it was a loving, quiet agreement. They complemented each other like two pieces of a puzzle that together formed a whole picture. Each had their own strengths, their own character, and yet they were inseparable.

After sixty years together, they renewed their vows, this time in the church in Vogelbach. It was a day full of love and gratitude for what they had built together. I was allowed to walk her down the aisle, and the Mainz court singers, friends of my father, sang in their honor. I gave a little speech, as I always do at family gatherings, and it was a moment that is indelibly etched onto my heart. It was proof that longlasting love really does exist, love that grows stronger even after decades, that continues to evolve, that endures throughout all the difficulties, laughter, and arguments.

My Father and I – A Bond For Life

His greatest joys were the births of his daughters. But he had a very special bond with me, his youngest. From the first moment, there was something between us that you can't explain; you can only feel it. Maybe it was because I was so similar to him. I was full of energy, curious, open-minded, and, just like him, a soccer fanatic. I started playing myself at an early age. My father was proud of me. And I was proud of him, not only because of his successes on the field, but above all because of his loyal, warm-hearted, humorous, and honest nature.

As he got older, our roles slowly shifted. He had always been there for me—and suddenly it was me who got to be there for him. I came with him to his appointments, events, and receptions. I became his manager, planned, organized, spoke for him when he no longer needed words, because we understood each other even without words. He often said to me: "When I leave this world, I know my legacy is in the best hands with you." And I knew how much that meant to him.

To me, he was never just the world champion, never just the soccer player. To me, he was my dad. My support, my role model, my home. And the fact that I carry him within me today—in my heart and in what I do—it is not because I have to continue something, but because I want to. Out of gratitude. Out of love. And because I gave him my promise that his story, his values, and his heart would live on in me.

The Wrong Eckel

It was one of those evenings when the phone rang and the mood in the house suddenly changed. My mother picked up, it was her sister Ilse. She was excited, out of breath, almost panicking. She burst out as soon as she had said hello: “Tell me, Hannelore, is it really true? Was Horst at that pub in town yesterday, buying champagne and sparkling wine rounds and flirting with random women?" My mother was totally shocked. “What are you talking about?” she asked, slightly annoyed. “Horst was home with me all day. All we did was assemble the cabinets and untangle the lamps.”

But aunt Ilse did not give up. She hadn't heard the story from just one person—rumors were spreading. Someone was seen in a disco or pub putting on quite a show, ordering champagne, handing out money, and flirting with women. And all this under the name of Horst Eckel. The man had actually claimed he was Horst Eckel. The world champion. My father. My mother was shocked. The idea that someone would simply appropriate her husband's name and use it to do something that was completely out of character for him was something she couldn't shake. Fortunately, the truth quickly emerged. My father had been at home the whole time that day, with my mother. So she was able to refute the story immediately. She knew with absolute certainty that there had been no champagne, if anything it would have been coffee. There had been no flirting, they had been assembling kitchen cabinets, together. No big show, just everyday family life.

The alleged witnesses had simply seen someone pretending to be Horst Eckel, presumably because he knew that the name would make an impression. And it obviously did just that. The man played the big shot, pretended to be a celebrity, ordered drinks generously, and threw money around. The real Horst Eckel would probably have thrown his hands up in horror at that moment, because that was not how he was at all. My mother was shocked at first, but she remained calm. She knew how quickly rumors could destroy careers, especially if the name is well-known. But she managed to stay calm because she knew what was really going on. The truth quickly came to light, and the story was soon debunked.

Nevertheless, this incident clearly demonstrated how fragile a reputation can be, how quickly people are to adorn themselves with a big name, how easily impressions arise that are based on nothing, and how important it is that there are people who know the difference between reality and pretense. In the end, no damage was done. My father's reputation was not sullied because those who really knew him did not doubt what was true and knew what was fabricated. And yet that evening stayed on my mother's mind for a long time. Not because she doubted him, but because she had to witness how carelessly others could treat a name that meant so much more to us than just an entry in the phone book.

To the End and Beyond

My parents were married their whole lives—from 1957. It wasn't a perfect, smooth Hollywood marriage; both of them were far too temperamental for that. They got into arguments more than once because they were both very stubborn. They argued loudly, they reconciled, they laughed, they cried. But they always stayed together. Their love was strong, honest, and full of life until the very last moment.

On December 3, 2021, my father passed away. It was up to me to break the sad news to my mother. When I told her, she just looked at me with those calm, knowing eyes. By then she was already ill, but she said very quietly: “Your father has passed away.” And I said: “Yes.” At that moment, I saw the greatest pain I have ever seen in a human being. It was as if a part of her went with him, just as a part of me went that day. But I knew that he would be waiting for her, that their love was stronger than death, stronger than any illness, any distance.

On October 12, 2024—not even three years after my father's death—my mother followed him. She died in my arms. But I don't think that was the end of their love. I believe that such love continues, even after death. That they found each other again and that they continue to dance, laugh, and sometimes argue a little, just as they always did. And that they know their love remains in our hearts, in the hearts of their grandchildren, their children, and grandchildren. Their love lives on—strong, quiet, and eternal.

As a token of their love, I had their two wedding bands and my mother's engagement ring remade into a single ring. I wear it on my hand, together with my grandmother's engagement ring. It is my memory of the people I love and of a love that overcame all obstacles, the love my parents had for each other. The most difficult and painful days of my life were both goodbyes and new beginnings—the time I had always feared when I would have to step up and accept my legacy. Those days have carved themselves deep into my heart, my soul, and my thoughts.

Horst Eckel
Born on February 8, 1932
Died on December 3, 2021

Hannelore Eckel
Born on February 2, 1937
Died on October 12, 2024

My parents.

A Decision to Love

My father was born at a time when childhood was not easy. When others were still playing with building blocks, he grew up in the shadow of an impending war. His family was poor, and he had had to do without many things. At the age of twelve, he had experienced what no child should ever experience: Air raid sirens, loss, fear, the emptiness after the impact. His older brother did not return home. The silence that followed in the family was deafening. Death did not pass through the village; it stayed. And with it the silence that henceforth overshadowed every meal, every conversation. A family that never completely healed.

Yet there was one place where his heart found relief: the soccer field. It was here that there was no war, no hunger, no loss. There he was just Horst, barefoot perhaps, but free. Soccer became his light, his refuge, his way of understanding the world and forgetting it for a moment.

At fifteen, the next blow came when his parents' marriage broke up. His brother had been killed in the war, his sister, eleven years older, was already married, but still lived in the house. He, the youngest, became his mother's rock. She had nothing but him. And he stayed. Although the door to a different life did open up—a new home with his father, a stepmother, a better education, a return to the secondary school he had previously had to leave because his mother couldn't afford it—he decided against it. He finished school, went to work at the sawmill, and labored hard with hands that had barely finished growing. He didn't stay because it was easy. He stayed because she needed him and because responsibility was not just a word to him, but his ethos.

When the greatest moment of his career came in 1954, he suddenly found himself at the center of the world's attention. He was Horst Eckel, the youngest member of the team, the "greyhound." He was a world champion in Bern. In a white jersey, with heart, with dignity, with a team that made history. And what did he do after the Miracle of Bern?

He took the money and renovated his mother's house. Not for fame, not for headlines. For her. To show his gratitude. Out of loyalty. But it was no use, because shortly afterward something happened that is difficult to put into words. His mother gave him a choice that wasn't really a choice. A decision as cruel as it was final. "It's either me or Hannelore. You can't have both." That was her ultimatum.

Hannelore, the girl he had known since she was three and he was eight. The girl from the sandbox who eventually became a woman. The love of his life. Hannelore Maria Schey, whom he affectionately called "Hanne." She wasn't just anyone, she was everything. His best friend, his confidant, his future.

But he was forced to choose between the past and the future. How does a young man decide at such a moment? Between the woman who gave birth to him and the one he wants to live with? It wasn't a case of either/or, it was an inner ripping apart. A mental test that would have broken many people. But my father decided. For love. For Hannelore. His mother disinherited him. He lost contact with his family of origin. The Eckel branch of the family became foreign to me, his daughter. I don't know my cousins; I never celebrated birthdays with my aunts or uncles on my father's side. The only part of the family I know is my mother's, the Scheys. That's the part that remained. My grandmother, my grandfather, my aunt Ilse, my cousin Irene, and my second cousin Cora.

My father and mother married in 1957. She was 20, my father 25. Their love wasn't like a fairy tale; it was real. Doors were slammed. Words were shouted. But they never left each other. We weren't a glamorous TV family, but one with heart, anger, laughter, and tears—just like in real life. And perhaps that's precisely what made it so special.

But life was to put my father to the test again. When he was 28 years old, he was faced with another decision that would change his life forever. It wasn't a decision about a game or a playing strategy, nor was it a substitution on the soccer field, but rather a choice between two paths in life. On one hand that of a professional soccer player at the highest level and on the other that of a man who chose his love, his wife, and his family.

It wasn't soccer that he left behind; that always remained a part of his life. It was his big dream of a having successful career as a national player that slipped away from him in that moment. Not because he couldn't have achieved it, but because the conditions for doing so were linked to something he couldn't commit to. There were people in his circle who had expectations of him. Expectations that would push him in a different direction, away from my mother, toward a life that would suit others.

However, as in his younger years, my father made his choice from the bottom of his heart. Titles, headlines, and a career meant nothing to him if they conflicted with what he loved. He decided against external pressure and in favor of the woman who had been by his side since childhood. For a life with her. For his family. And so he chose the more difficult but more sincere path.

The exact reasons, circumstances, and individuals involved are part of our family's unspoken history. They will stay with me. Not because they should remain hidden, but because they deserve to be protected for what they once were. I don't want to harm anyone. Just show what it meant, what my father did. That love sometimes requires more courage than any final moment in a stadium full of lights. And that in moments like these, you realize who someone really is.

But he never left soccer, or rather, soccer never left him. My father played until he was in his 80s. Not because he was looking for fame, but because soccer was part of his soul. He was not a former player. He was always a soccer player.

Why am I telling this story?

Because it was never told. Because the public only knows the image of the world champion. The medal, the pats on the back, the man in black-and-white pictures. But not the son who went to the sawmill at fifteen. Not the brother who was hurt by loss. Not the man who opted out of the easier life, who left the golden path for what he truly loved.

I tell it because people deserve the truth. Not the fairy tale, because my father was not only a hero, but also a human being. A father. A man with flaws, with courage, with heart. Because I love him. And because I carry his legacy, because the public has always formed an image of me that is not true. The world champion's daughter—that's how people see me. But hardly anyone asks: Who are you really? Only a few see the woman behind the label, her own story, the struggles that I also face. I'm not just the daughter of a famous man.

I am his daughter. And that means I carry his courage. His decisions. His humanity. And his love.

My Dad And I

The bond between my father and me began before I was born. Some relationships don't start with a first look or a first smile, but with an unspoken feeling—a premonition, a quiet promise that weaves itself between two souls before words and gestures ever take hold. That's how it was with my father and me. Our story didn't begin on the day I was born, but much earlier.

My mother had always dreamed of having children, but the path to getting there was anything but easy. She suffered several miscarriages, which took a severe toll on her, not just physically but emotionally as well. I believe it was this experience that gave her the persistent feeling that happiness is fragile and could slip away at any moment. Shortly before becoming pregnant with me, she had suffered another miscarriage. The doctor told her definitively, "It is absolutely impossible for you to get pregnant in the next four weeks." But life, especially when it comes to me, had other plans. I was already there, in the smallest of beginnings, quiet and determined.

One day, my parents were out walking in Kaiserslautern. As they browsed the shops, my mother was suddenly overcome with an intense craving for tomatoes. She bought a whole bag and ate them right then and there. My father watched this, and as was typical when Hanne indulged her little quirks, he was surprised but didn't say a word. Later, at home, my mother felt terribly nauseous. She sat on the top step, clutching her stomach, and thought, "How can you want children this badly and feel so miserably sick at the same time?" But deep down, she already knew.

My father was skeptical at first when she went to the doctor the next day. But the impossible became possible: I was on my way. Even before I was born, I had a mind of my own, a will of my own. My mother often said with a laugh, "You already asserted yourself back then." The doctor who heard the heartbeat—strong and powerful—was convinced until the end: "It's going to be a boy." My baby booklet was light blue, and my parents chose names. Joachim or Peter. But my father could hardly pronounce "Joachim," so they decided on Peter. But then came a memorable evening.

How I got my name

Two days before I was born, my parents were sitting in front of the TV in the living room. Everything seemed normal until my father—who never said things like this out of the blue—suddenly said, "Hey, Hanne... what if it's a girl after all?" My mother looked at him, surprised: "Now what makes you think that? The doctor said it's going to be a boy." But my father insisted: "I have a feeling..." And just at that moment, Dagmar Berghoff appeared on TV. She was an iconic presence at the time, announcing the next program in a calm tone of voice. My mother laughed: "Dagmar is a beautiful name." My father nodded: "Yes, Dagmar... that's beautiful." But my mother, was still undecided. "Or Annette?" But then my father interjected: "Annette? But that's the name of Renate's daughter!" Renate was my mother's best friend, and the idea that her daughter and I could have the same name was unthinkable for my father. Finally, they agreed: Dagmar Annette Eckel.

As my mother often recounted, a tender bond formed at that very moment. My father, who had always been quite serious and practical, revealed for the first time that he already felt a sense of responsibility, love, and affection for the little one on the way. Before that, however, there was a darker memory—the one involving the bottle of schnapps.

My mother was worried. Deeply worried. She was afraid my father wouldn't love their second child—me—as much as the first. She had doubts. There was even an argument one night, when he came home late, shortly before I was born. Maybe it was a mix of anger, disappointment, fear, and a nagging uncertainty that made her sit down at the kitchen table with a bottle of schnapps and a glass. She poured herself a drink, holding the glass with a tremor, almost as a silent question: Will he say anything? Will he even notice? When my father got home, he saw the scene and got angry. Not the kind of anger that's loud and slams doors, but that deep, fundamental anger that shows the issue is bigger than just the moment.

He poured the glass and the bottle down the drain, his expression serious. "Hanne, how could you? This is dangerous for you and the baby!" And in that moment, my mother knew: He loved me. He loved this child. He cared. She never told him that directly, but she told me again and again, as proof that love is sometimes found not in words but in actions.

And then the day of my birth arrived. My mother was in labor, and my father drove her to the hospital. Again, he thought, just as he had with my sister, "Oh, it'll still be a while." He wanted to go home again—maybe play some soccer, kill some time. But the nurse stopped him: "Mr. Eckel, stay here! She's already ten centimeters dilated. It won't be long now." My father just laughed: "They told me that the first time, too." And he actually drove home.

He had just arrived home when the phone rang. It was the hospital. I had been born. It was only a twenty-minute drive, but suddenly he had to turn around and rush back to the hospital, back to me. When he arrived, my mother placed me in his arms. "Here, look," she said, "she looks like an Eckel." My father looked at me and smiled. "She actually looks more like the eldest," he said. But then he added quietly, "You know, sometimes it's not just about looks; it's about character." He couldn't have known then that my personality was as similar to his as my appearance. Later, I would joke, "Dad, you can't deny I'm yours." And he would grin back, "No, first of all, I wouldn't want to, and second, I truly couldn't."

And there he stood, holding me in his arms, this tiny new life. My mother felt a huge weight lift from her heart. She knew in that moment that the bond between my father and me had been strong, deep, and unbreakable right from the start.

So, my name is Dagmar Eckel. I was born on May 21, 1968, and I had a light blue baby booklet. And I had a bond with my parents—especially my father—that has never broken since. It was a bond stronger than words, one that endured through all the ups and downs, and it lives on in me to this day.

When I was finally born, I didn't look as much like my father as everyone had expected. I had black hair right away—not a lot, but enough that my mother combed it up into a little cap. I was very dark overall, almost exotic compared to my blonde sister. And in the first few days after my birth, I actually had long black hair on my forehead, chest, and even my back. My sister thought this was hilarious and immediately nicknamed me "monkey." But that wasn't all. Because my grandmother Käthe, my grandfather's second wife, wanted to help my sister remember my name, she explained that the beginning of Dagmar was like "Dackel" (German for dachshund), the neighbor's dog, and the rest was like her friend "Marie." And so, I simply became "Dackel Marie" to my sister and I kept that name for quite a while.

Fortunately, my long hair gradually fell out—the "little monkey" slowly turned into a normal baby. But I kept my slightly darker skin tone, at least in the summer when I was outside and tanned quickly. Incidentally, my first word was—of course—"Mama." But "Papa" followed shortly after, and then, very typically for our family, the word "ball." Just like my father, I was athletic and active from a young age. I was already walking at eleven months and loved playing with a ball. It was clear that I had inherited his athleticism. But it was above all our shared character that connected us so strongly.

Our little secrets

From the very beginning, we shared many things: a love of soccer, a love of exercise, and sports in general. But our little secrets, which my mother only learned about many years later, brought us even closer. Secrets full of childlike joy and trust, of adventures that belonged only to the two of us.

One of these secrets started when I was about three years old. My father played and coached soccer in addition to his work as a teacher. One day, he took me to one of his games. That was the most wonderful thing for me. I felt like I belonged, like I was stepping into a world full of adventure and community. On the way home, he let me sit on his lap. The roads weren't as busy back then as they are today, and my father let me hold the steering wheel. Of course, he was in control, but I got to steer—at least a little bit. I felt fantastic and free, as if I were the driver myself. He just said, "But you mustn't tell Mommy." And I, as the good little secret-keeper, solemnly promised, "No, I won't!" And I never did tell her. It wasn't until many years later, when I was an adult, that I told my mother this story, and she laughed about how we had kept our little secrets.

My father was usually very meticulous about his car; every scratch was a thorn in his side. But at that moment, as I sat on his lap and held the steering wheel, he didn't care. He trusted me. And I felt how he protected me, how he took me into this little world of "adults" with a mixture of adventurousness and care. That moment was very special to me.

These little moments, when I felt that my father trusted me, and that I was "his little girl," they shaped our relationship. We laughed a lot, we shared these silent conspiracies, little "you and me against the rest of the world" moments. And even when things got difficult later in life, this foundation, this deep, loving bond between us, always remained. These little secrets and adventures with my father were very special, but not all car rides with him were so fun and carefree. There were also moments that were less glamorous and somewhat "unusual."

The legend of the fur coat

I was about four years old when my grandmother Käthe visited us. It was a cozy evening, and we were having spinach for dinner. Well, "cozy" was a very relative term for me, because spinach was definitely not my favorite dish, to put it mildly. But as was the custom in our family, we had to clean our plates. So I bravely chewed the greenish mush that felt like wet grass in my mouth. I swallowed it down—what choice did I have?

After dinner, it was time for my father to drive my grandmother home. Grandma Käthe was quite proud of herself, especially her fur coat. Back then, it was a status symbol, a sign of elegance. Today, of course, I'd give her an earful—animal testing and fur coats are simply unacceptable! But in those days... well, that's just how things were. And Grandma Käthe wore that coat with her head held high and an air that said, "I am the queen of the family."

We got in the car. Grandma was in the front passenger seat in her stylish fur coat, and my father was at the wheel. He was always a dynamic driver who liked to take the curves a little faster. I sat in the back. That's when it hit me: these curves, all that spinach, the motion... It was a terrible mix. I felt ill. Really ill. My stomach was churning, and I thought I felt my face turn green.

I leaned forward, wanting to say, "Dad, I don't feel...," but it was already too late. The spinach came back out with a vengeance. In a graceful arc, the entire contents of my little stomach flew forward, landing directly on the collar of my grandmother's elegant fur coat. The green mush seeped into the collar, ran down her back, and left a clearly visible trail of "spinach art." Nobody ever forgot that moment.

Grandma Käthe was horrified. Her beloved fur coat was ruined! My father gripped the steering wheel, probably in shock, trying to keep the car from crashing into a ditch. I sat in the back, pale and guilty, thinking only, I hope we get home soon... Despite everything, we made it. Fortunately, the fur coat could be cleaned, and my grandmother eventually calmed down after the initial shock. I never suffered from motion sickness that badly again. It was probably a one-off, albeit spectacular, incident. Today we all laugh about it. But back then... Well, I'd say I created my very own, unique "spinach legend" that evening. My father would later tell the story with a wink about how his little Dagmar broke all records while eating spinach and riding in the car.

Why I didn't become a soccer player

At the age of twelve, I was a total tomboy—no question about it. I wanted to be like a boy and felt like one, too. I quickly noticed that boys seemed to have more freedom than girls. So I thought, Why should I follow the rules when I could just as easily live life as a boy? The answer: I could, and all I really wanted was to play soccer!

That's when my mother got involved, of course. She had her own ideas about what her daughter should be. My grades needed to be good, and sports came second. She actually forbade me from playing soccer seriously because she didn't think it was "womanly" enough for a girl. Sure, school was the most important thing in her view, but I just couldn't help myself. Soccer was pure joy for me.

Finally, one afternoon I got the chance to really play. I secretly joined a game with the boys. One nasty fall and I landed hard on my arm and immediately felt that something was wrong. Oh, great, I thought to myself. That wasn't supposed to happen, but hey, it's all part of the game. When my father picked me up from the field, he was typically dramatic: "Oh dear, you're going to be in big trouble at home." But he himself took it relatively easy, of course. What I didn't realize was that my arm had already started to turn into a real work of art—blue and swollen like a balloon. At home, my mother took a closer look at my arm and, after a moment's hesitation, decided we should go to the hospital.

Then came the shock at the hospital: my arm was put in a cast at a right angle! I now looked like a walking geometry experiment. But well, what could I do? With one arm fixed at a right angle to my body, I could hardly do anything. Luckily, my other hand was just as dexterous as my right, so at least I could still brush my teeth and use the toilet. But that was about it in terms of practical advantages. For everything else, I had to rely on my family's help.

I was now only allowed to sit in the corner with a cast on my arm and wait for the next big thing to come along in my life, something that didn't involve a cast or broken bones. But the real fun began afterwards: when I finally got rid of the cast, my mother took it as proof that soccer wasn't for me and forbade me from playing. She said it was too dangerous and that I should focus on my school grades.

My soccer career was officially over—without any spectacular goals or victories, but at least I now had a story to tell and the knowledge that, at the age of twelve, I already had the "coolest cast" of the year. As luck would have it, my father never stopped raving about my "missed career" as a soccer player. Even though my great future as a soccer player never came true, at least my time as "Ronny" in soccer was unbeatable—albeit only for a short time.

The chin scar family

I was about nine or ten years old and—as my mother always so affectionately put it—a real tomboy. Short hair, usually dressed in boys' clothes, conquering the world outside, fearless and always full of energy. On this particular day, I had set my mind on performing a very special feat: I wanted to prove that I was the undisputed queen of balance.

Back then, we still had my grandparents' old kitchen. It was a kitchen straight out of an old family movie: a tall, old cupboard, in front of it a solid kitchen table, and in front of that, wobbly chairs. For me, it wasn't just a kitchen, it was my personal circus and adventure playground! So I stood fearlessly between the cupboard and a chair, one hand firmly on the backrest, the other on the cupboard. Then I started to rock. Carefully at first—back and forth, back and forth. My mother gave me that typical warning look and called out sternly, "You'd better not do that!" But my father—oh, my dad—stood nearby, smiled, and said with that familiar twinkle in his eyes, "Oh, let her be."

That was my cue. Higher, even more daring! I rocked, laughed, and felt like a circus acrobat in the ring. Until—bang!—my feet were suddenly above my head. I tipped forward, lost my balance, and slammed my chin full force onto the kitchen floor.

I can still remember exactly how I reflexively pressed my hand to my face, as if I could make the mishap invisible. "No, everything's fine!" I muttered bravely as my parents came running. But unfortunately, everything was not fine—blood was already dripping onto the floor from between my fingers. My father quickly sat me down on his lap in the living room, carefully moved my hand away from my chin, took a look at it, and said with a grin, "Oh my goodness, look, it's a real hole—you can almost see through it to your teeth!" Great. That was a comforting diagnosis. We drove straight to the hospital. I bravely endured the injections and stitches, and as a reward I got a band-aid and—best of all—a day off school! When I got home, I looked at the little scar on my chin, almost with pride: I was now officially a member of the chin scar family.

My father had had the famous Eckel scar for a long time. He told me that he had gotten it as a young man when a shoe had hit him on the foot. The momentum had caused him to stumble, and he had hit the ground with his chin. And my mother wore her scar as a souvenir of an unfortunate fall in her childhood. I now continued the family tradition after my swing adventures.

But that wasn't all. After we got back, my father sat me on his lap, took me in his arms, and began—with his typical mix of mischief and love—to tell me one of his stories. "Imagine this," he said with a grin, "I used to follow your mother around on my little Vespa scooter when she was young. She had a date, and I wanted to know what she was up to!" I giggled, picturing my dad hiding behind a street corner on his Vespa, and almost forgot the throbbing pain in my chin. It was one of those moments that show a child how much their parents love them. When they are there for you, when they comfort you, when they take you in their arms with stories, laughter, and all their warmth.

And every time I feel the small scar on my chin today, I am reminded of that day—the swinging in the old kitchen, the fall, the blood, the scar, the stories, the laughter. I am reminded of my father, who said with a twinkle in his eye, "Oh, let her be." All I can say is: if you're going to get a cut on your chin, then please do it as a member of the Eckel family's traditional scar collection!

The dining room story, or how Dad and I discovered the art of small theater

It was one of those days when the whole family gathered around what seemed like a minor incident. To this day, I don't remember exactly what I had done, probably just knocked over a glass of water or something similarly insignificant. But my mother and grandmother turned it into a Shakespearean drama, culminating in a barrage of admonitions. I, young and yet already a little rebel at heart, openly contradicted my mother and grandmother for the first time in my life.

My father, who had been watching the whole thing from a distance, had remained silent at first. But at some point, as I continued to disagree, he lost his temper, or rather, he decided it was time for one of his famous, unforgettable interventions. With a serious expression on his face, he grabbed me by the arm and marched me into the dining room. The dining room was right next to the kitchen, so my mother and grandmother could follow every move. "Right, now I'm going to put you over my knee," he thundered in a deep voice as he closed the door behind us. "Maybe then you'll change your mind about what happened!"

Outside the door, you could hear frightened gasps. My mother and grandmother stood frozen, hands clasped, staring at the door as if they might have to jump in and intervene at any moment. I, on the other hand, stood there with wide, round eyes, my heart pounding wildly, until I saw the tiny, familiar spark in my dad's eyes. There it was, that very special twinkle that only he had, that grin that always meant, "Come along, this will be fun."

And then the little drama began: with a serious face, but the corners of his mouth twitching, my father slapped the soft, burgundy leather chairs, which, with their ornate carvings, were the showpiece of the dining room. "Ouch, ouch! That hurts! I didn't do anything!" I cried loudly, playing my part with growing enthusiasm. From outside, we heard a soft whimper that slowly grew louder. "Horst, stop! Don't hit her! Don't put her over your knee! It wasn't that big of a deal!" came the desperate cry through the door. The concern of the two women outside the door—my mother and my grandmother—was simply too delicious. My father once again prepared to dramatically slap the chair, while I could hardly contain my laughter. Soon we were both lying half on the floor, completely out of breath from giggling, while outside there was still whispering, whimpering, and praying.

But then, when my grandmother finally burst into tears, we decided to end the spectacle. We opened the door—and there they stood: my mother and grandmother, with tear-stained eyes, clasped hands, and worry on their faces. At first, they stared at me in disbelief as I stood there with red cheeks and eyes sparkling from laughter. But slowly it dawned on them that the whole thing had been just a loving, tongue-in-cheek performance between my father and me.

At first, there was great indignation, especially from my grandmother, who sulked for the rest of the day. My mother was also less than enthusiastic about our little performance. But years later—at family gatherings or simply on cozy evenings—this story was brought up again and again. It became a symbol of the special humor my father and I shared and of the loving bond between us, which always had room for a wink even in serious moments.

Alone in the stadium with a lot of confidence

Like so many days, this one in 1978 was very special. When I was ten years old, my father took me to a soccer game. Not just anywhere—no, to Betzenberg, to his FC Kaiserslautern. To him, the stadium was more than just a place, it was a piece of his soul. When he talked about it, his eyes lit up and his voice took on that special tone, a little wistful, a little proud, as if he were talking about an old home he had never left.

Now I, his little darling, was officially allowed to be there. I remember wearing my jacket with the sewn-on buttons and my red FC Kaiserslautern scarf, which was almost as long as I was tall. We walked through the stadium's gate, and I immediately sensed that everything was different here. It was loud, lively, vibrant, as if the concrete itself had a heartbeat. I sat on my dad's lap, right in the middle of the old grandstand, where the plaster had seen a few decades and the wind mingled with the smell of bratwurst and beer. Next to us sat his friends, men with names that would later spell soccer history. At the time, to me they were just "the men with the firm hands and loud voices." They shouted things like "Cover him!" and "He's offside!" I understood exactly what was happening on the field. I was only ten, but I loved the ball, I understood the game, and I loved seeing my father like that. Upright, proud, and full of life.

The game was explosive. My father cheered, jumped up, shouted things like "There it is!" and I jumped too, even though I didn't know exactly what he was talking about because the ball was already somewhere else. But it didn't matter, I was there. I was part of it. One heartbeat with thousands of others. When the final whistle blew and FC Kaiserslautern had won, my father was in high spirits. He grinned, shook hands, and was greeted from all sides like an old captain who was back on board. Then he leaned down to me, looked at me with that mischievous look he always had when he thought nothing was about to happen, even though something was already happening, and said, "Sweetheart, stay here. I'm just going to the VIP room to have a beer with the boys. I'll be right back."

I nodded. Of course I remained seated. I was his little darling, after all. And when daddy said something, it was the law. So I sat there, all alone among a few thousand empty seats that still felt a little bit like they were moving, like a sea that had just calmed down. People streamed out of the stadium, laughing, shouting, some still singing. Then it got quieter. A few cleaners came through with brooms, collected cups, and shoved trash into large plastic bags. I dangled my legs, rocked back and forth a little, and thought nothing of it. I waited because I knew my dad would be back soon. But then it slowly became really quiet. The wind blew through the stands. The stadium lights flickered a little. And for the first time, I had the feeling that something might be wrong. Maybe he had forgotten me?

I stood up, a little hesitantly, and went to the large door of the VIP room and knocked. A tall man with a serious expression and a radio on his belt opened the door.

"Well, what are you doing here?"

"I'm looking for my dad."

"And who is your dad?"

"Horst Eckel."

He frowned. "Wait a minute."

And he disappeared. I stood there, my scarf dangling down to my knees, my heart beating faster than it should. When he came back, he looked at me sympathetically: "Well, your dad... he's already gone. He drove home."

I stood there. Frozen. Me? Alone? In the stadium? And he was just... gone?

"Can I maybe stay here until he comes back?"

"I'm sorry, that's not possible. You'd better go back to your seat."

So I went back. And sat down in my seat again. I did what he said. I waited. I wasn't sad. Not even angry. I was just... confident, because I knew he would come back. It wasn't a question of if, only when. And then, out of nowhere, I heard quick footsteps. First quiet, then louder. Then heavy breathing. And suddenly he came shooting around the corner—my dad. His hair was tousled, his face red, and he was completely out of breath. When he saw me, his arms flew up like an airplane coming in for a landing. He picked me up, hugged me tight, and said, "Sweetie! I'm so sorry! I was already home! I was standing at the door with the key and then I thought: Something's missing! And then it dawned on me... YOU!"

I looked at him. I wanted to laugh and cry at the same time. "Dad, I just waited. You told me to stay here. I knew you'd come." He looked at me as if I were the smartest kid in the world. Maybe I was, at that moment. "I broke every speed record on the way back," he muttered. "If the police had caught me, I wouldn't have cared. The main thing is that you're here."

We drove home, silent but filled with warmth. The car smelled of his cologne, stadium air, and a hint of guilt. I leaned my head on his shoulder and closed my eyes. We didn't tell my mother until many years later. At first she was horrified, but then she laughed. And she told the story herself at every opportunity. I will never forget how I sat there. Ten years old. All alone in the stadium. And completely certain in my heart: He's coming. He said so. And I believed him. That's exactly why this was never a story about my father forgetting me, but a story about me trusting him. And about him racing back in record time with screeching tires and an open heart. A small eternity on the Betzenberg and the most beautiful proof of how great trust can be.

“Tennis racket day”

It was the summer of 1982, and I was fourteen years old. Tennis wasn’t necessarily my great passion. I enjoyed playing tennis, yes, but in recent years I hadn’t had the chance to play. Nevertheless, I decided with great enthusiasm to make the most of my abilities. Of course, my first thought was: “I want to join the same tennis club as my father!” Where else but there should I start my career as a future queen of tennis?

So I joined the club where my father had been a member for years. It was a mixture of “father-daughter day” and “I’ll try to outdo everyone and anything” on the court. But as luck would have it, I also ended up in a group with three friends who also played tennis. There were four of us, and it was supposed to be a relaxed afternoon full of rallies and sunshine. My father, who taught tennis, had other ideas of course. The other girls were allowed to happily make their mistakes without him commenting on them too much. Mistakes? No problem. Everyone was equal—except me. Because I was “his daughter,” and he knew what I was capable of—I had talent. So he expected me to prove it with every stroke. No mistakes, no weaknesses, no excuses.

I didn’t understand that right away. When all the other girls tried to hit the ball and regularly missed, he nodded understandingly and said, “It’s okay, that can happen, it’s just part of the game.” But when I made a mistake, there were no excuses. My father’s looks said more than a thousand words. This created an almost unstoppable temper in me that bubbled like a volcano in a young teenager.

One beautiful summer day, when I had once again made a particularly “unforgivable” mistake, I lost my temper. I grabbed my tennis racket and flung it across the entire court, as if it were an angry thunderbolt. There, he had it! I was furious. My father, who was probably as surprised by this tennis tantrum as a squirrel falling into a spoonful of honey, immediately called an end to the training session. The other girls, who had just been laughing at a failed serve, were quickly dismissed.

Now there we stood, he and I, and I desperately tried to control my anger. "Why did you react like that?" he asked with a wink as we stood facing each other. "Was that really necessary?"

I stared at him and said, "Well, maybe I overreacted, but it really annoyed me! You always praise the others, even when they make the same mistakes I do! Why can't I make mistakes too?" And then came the big moment—the redeeming words that somehow calmed me down, even though they weren't what I had expected. He put his hand on my shoulder and said, "Honey, I train the others here, but you're my daughter. I see what you're capable of, and that's why I expect more from you." I looked at him, and even though I was still a little mad, I understood what he meant. He just wanted to get the best out of me. And yes, okay, maybe it wasn't the smartest move to use the tennis racket as my personal weapon of protest. But at that moment, it was the only way I could show him that I had my own expectations and desires too. And, surprise, surprise, he actually understood.

We laughed together and the rest of the training session was—well—a little more relaxed. I was able to think clearly again and began to really understand the lesson: mistakes are okay, but you should always believe in yourself and not let anger about unfairness paralyze you. I continued to play tennis, less later on because I didn't have much time for it, but I would never forget the "tennis racket day" that taught me that sometimes you just need a break to reflect on yourself, and to also annoy your father a little. But as he told me later again and again, that was the moment he knew I was going to be something really big—provided, of course, that I was able to refrain from throwing my racket every time I made a small mistake.

The secret agent in the living room

That same year, in the midst of puberty, with all the little excitements that go with it, I had a visit in the afternoon from a boy I really liked. Not a steady boyfriend, nothing official, but someone who had turned my head a little, as happens when you're fourteen. We sat in the kitchen, drank coffee, and talked about this and that. It was harmless, completely normal—for me, anyway. But for my father, it was an alarm signal that activated his inner secret agent. He knew exactly what was going on. Fathers notice these things. And so, that afternoon, Operation Kitchen Surveillance began.

My father sat in the living room, pretending to be relaxing as he watched a soccer match. But of course, he had his ears everywhere. After a while, he got up, seemingly inconspicuously, and walked into the kitchen. "I'm just going to get a quick coffee," he said, as if that were the normal afternoon plan. But what followed was nothing short of a mini theatrical performance. He prepared his coffee with such meticulous care, as if operating a highly complex machine. He measured out the water drop by drop, scooped out the individual coffee grounds, and inserted the filter so deliberately that I thought he was about to earn a Ph.D. in the art of the barista. As the machine finally began to bubble, he gave us that very special look—the "I'm here and I see everything" look that fathers have perfected when their daughter is sitting in the kitchen with a boy.

Finally finished, he pretended to retreat to the living room. But less than five minutes later—poof!—he was back. "I forgot the milk," he said with such calmness, as if it were the most natural thing in the world. So he opened the fridge, fished out the milk, carefully poured it into the cup, and gave us that "watch out, I'm here" look again. I blushed slightly, trying to suppress my nervous laughter, while my crush, the boy I really liked, looked at me, slightly unsettled. "Is this normal for you guys?" his eyes seemed to ask. I nodded almost imperceptibly and whispered quietly, "Just wait, that was only the beginning."

After the milk incident, which took longer than a three-course meal, the next act followed: my father came back, this time with the excuse that he was hungry. "After all that hard work making coffee, you need something proper to eat," he said, again, as if it were the most natural thing in the world. So he started to prepare a snack. Each motion was a meticulous performance. Butter was portioned with precision, and the jam jar was opened as if to reveal a hidden gem. The spoon plunged in, spreading jam onto the bread with surgical precision. Amidst this silent focus, the gentle clink of spoons and clatter of cups provided a counterpoint, along with the hushed drone of the TV—soccer, naturally—a soundtrack seemingly meant to blend into the background.

We were still sitting there, my cheeks burning bright red and a nervous giggle escaping me, while my father meticulously monitored our every move as part of his self-assigned surveillance mission. After the snack, the inevitable cleanup followed. He simply couldn't leave the plates and cups sitting out. So, he went back into the kitchen, collected everything with exaggerated care, clinked the cutlery, and made so much noise that even the neighbors must have known the world's strictest supervision was currently active in our kitchen. The boy was visibly nervous now. "Tell me, is your father always like this?" he whispered. I sighed and grinned. "Only when I like someone."

Finally, I couldn't hold back any longer. I leaned toward him and whispered, "You'd better leave now, before my father comes up with a new mission..." We got up, politely thanked him for the coffee, which was like a scene in a spy thriller, and headed for the door. My father was sitting in the living room, completely relaxed, his legs casually crossed, the TV on, and he looked at us with a gaze that clearly said, "Mission accomplished. No more danger."

I knew right then and there: my father wasn't just a loving dad. He was also the head of all agents—armed with humor, a mischievous grin, and a heart that never stopped protecting me, even though I was already fourteen and had a crush on a boy. I'm sure the boy never forgot that afternoon, and he never had coffee with us again. I still remember that afternoon with a smile. My dad, the best kitchen secret agent in the world.

The umbrella of terror

It was 1984, I was sixteen years old, and it was Carnival season. I remember exactly the cheerful atmosphere, the colorful costumes, the laughter, and the tingling sensation I felt when I had this one boy by my side. Not a steady boyfriend, nothing serious, but I liked him—as you do when you're sixteen. We were at a Carnival event very close to our hometown, laughing, talking, and at some point the evening came to an end. Since I didn't have a driver's license yet, this nice boy drove me home—a completely harmless, friendly gesture. We stood in front of my front door, chatted a bit, said our good nights. It was a beautiful moment, until it wasn't.

Behind the frosted glass pane of our front door, the light suddenly flickered on. The slightly yellowish light that always came on when someone was in the hallway. At that moment, I knew: dad was there. A shadow appeared behind the glass, grew larger, and then the door swung open. My father stood in the doorway like a guard, holding an umbrella aloft like a sword, his other hand casually resting on his hip. I swear, at that moment he looked like the hero in an old swashbuckling movie, only with an umbrella instead of a sword.

The poor boy next to me froze as if he had seen a ghost. I heard only an "Oh!" followed by a loud "Ah!", and then he was gone. Just gone. He ran faster than I believed a human being could run. It was as if he was arocket. I stood there, the door half open, my heart pounding, not knowing whether to laugh or sink into the ground. My father, still armed with the umbrella, turned to me with a grin and said dryly, "That young lad is quite jumpy. But he can run!" Then he lowered the umbrella as if he were a victorious knight and calmly walked back into the kitchen. I stood there, still half in shock, but also amused, when I heard my father begin his story as soon as he reached the kitchen. "You won't believe what just happened!" I heard him exclaim as he sat down at the kitchen table with a dramatic sigh. I knew that my mother and the rest of the family would burst out laughing.

"I saw the two of them at the door," he said in his best storytelling voice. "I had to check that everything was okay. So I grabbed my umbrella—you never know! And when I opened the door, there was the guy—as if he was about to walk right in! But I showed him!" I crept quietly into the kitchen, blushing slightly as my mother shook her head, smiling. My family giggled, and I knew that this would be another story shared at family gatherings.

It wasn't exactly the most glorious evening of my life, but it was one of the funniest and proof that my father always looked out for me. Even if it was a bit over the top sometimes. The boy never came back to visit, but I'm sure he told his friends this story for years to come: about the father who burst through the door armed with an umbrella, and chased him away. I still remember it today with a big grin and fond thoughts of my dad.

The unforgettable visits to Switzerland

Another story that always brings a smile to my face is one of our legendary "Switzerland trips" that are unforgettable not only because of the beautiful landscape, but above all because of the curious circumstances and special encounters.

This time, it was about nothing less than the famous Wankdorf Stadium. The legendary stadium in Bern was to be demolished and rebuilt. But the iconic clock of the Wankdorf Stadium, which had timed so many unforgettable moments, was to be preserved at all costs. It was to continue ticking in the new stadium to keep up tradition. The clock had been manufactured by the renowned Swiss watch brand Longines, known for its reliability and precision, and was a true symbol of the "Miracle of Bern."

We made our way to Switzerland to attend a meeting with the people in charge at Longines. They had manufactured the famous clock back in the day and were now to take it over for the new stadium construction. The meeting was special because Peter Lohmeyer, actor, soccer fan, and just a cool guy, was also there. He was one of the leading actors in the musical "The Miracle of Bern." We all sat together at a long table in the hotel bar, telling stories, drinking wine, laughing a lot, and enjoying the evening. At some point, Lohmeyer had to leave. He said a charming goodbye, left a few casual remarks, and disappeared into the night. I, on the other hand, wanted to stay a little longer and continue talking to the Longines representative. After all, the whole thing was exciting—a piece of soccer history!

Meanwhile, my father sat with us at the hotel bar. Although I was already in my mid-twenties and theoretically could have been traveling alone in Switzerland, he remained seated. Again and again he said quietly, "I'm going up to the room." But he stayed put. He ordered another drink, listened, laughed at the stories and, kept an eye on me. He kept toying with the idea of going up, but in the end he just sat there at the hotel bar until I eventually was tired from the long journey, the conversations, and the good wine. I ended the conversation and said, "All right, I'll go upstairs now."

It was his own quiet, loving trick: he didn't have to persuade me at all. He just waited, gave me my freedom, and was there when I got tired and ended the conversation. Very charming, very unobtrusive, but with that wonderful fatherly instinct that said, "I'll stay here until I'm sure you're safe." Of course, we also talked about the Wankdorf Stadium again on this occasion. My father grinned: "Well, the old stadium is being demolished, but the clock will remain. Always punctual, always reliable. Just like me." I laughed: "Yes, and always keeping an eye on your daughter, right?" He smiled: "Of course, who else?"

I still remember that scene to this day. Not only because of the Wankdorf Stadium and the famous Longines clock, but because of the special way in which my father, despite me having long grown up, always remained in the background with his fatherly care. He was simply there. And that was what counted.

There was also a visit to Switzerland with all the grandchildren and descendants of the 1954 World Cup winners. My father was the only World Cup winner still alive at the time. It was an unforgettable experience for me, as I was able to share it with my father. And my daughter was there, she was only one year old, but at least the generation was represented. I sat with my father in the garden of the Hotel Belvedere, enjoying a moment of silence. Then he suddenly asked me, "Can you hear them?" I nodded, even though at first I didn't know exactly what he meant. But then, as if by magic, I began to hear them too—the voices. The laughter, the conversations, the games. It was as if the walls of the room had opened up and I could hear the men who had brought the World Cup title to Germany back in the 1950s. The voices of his teammates, as if they were still among us. I can see them too," I said, and suddenly it was as if time had turned back. We sat there, both gazing into the distance, and for a brief, magical moment, it was as if the team were complete again. It was a wonderful experience, a connection between past and present, between the years and the memories.

It was more than just a walk through the garden. It was a step into the past, a look back at everything he and his comrades had experienced together. It was the moment when I felt the quiet sadness my father carried within him, but also the deep gratitude for the time they had spent together. And above all, gratitude for the fact that I was able to share this time with him, that I was there when he once again heard his team, felt his friends and comrades in the distance.

After sitting there for a while, we decided to go to the lake together. It was a beautiful walk, and I could see my father saying goodbye to his comrades. It was a quiet farewell, but one that said so much more than words ever could. Today, when I think back on that encounter, it still brings tears to my eyes.

This experience showed me how deep the connection between him and the other heroes of Bern really was. It is a memory that will stay with me forever, as will the story of these men who made history and will live on forever in people's hearts. That was the moment I vowed to myself that I would never give up this memory of these men and would always fight for it. It was a once-in-a-lifetime moment, a moment that deepened the bond between me and my father in a way that no words could ever describe. In that moment, I felt not only my father's love and understanding for me, but also my love and deep understanding for him. It is a memory that will connect us both forever.

Hamburg, the premiere, and the red carpet

It was a special, unique evening: the premiere of the musical "The Miracle of Bern" in Hamburg. And I was there. Not as a mere guest or spectator, but as the daughter of a man who had actually lived through this miracle. My father, Horst Eckel, the last surviving hero of 1954, and me, his daughter, who accompanied him because I knew that even a world champion is sometimes just a person who doesn't want to be alone. My father was involved in the filming as a consultant for the screenwriter and for the play's director.

He had grown older, but his spirit was still the same as it was back then when he stood on the field and made history with his teammates. He was really looking forward to this performance, to the musical that would tell his story and that of his friends. I remember exactly how we drove to Hamburg together—him, excited like a little boy, me, full of pride, and with that slight lump in my throat that you get when you know something very special is going to happen.

When we arrived at the theater, the atmosphere was electric. Flashbulbs, cameras, reporters, curious glances everywhere. The red carpet was rolled out, and I, the daughter of a world champion, was allowed to walk on it with him. I had dressed up especially for the occasion: a long, beautiful, flattering dress that I had chosen for this special occasion. A little glamour, a little elegance. After all, it was supposed to be an evening full of glamour and memories.

But as soon as we arrived, my father intervened, so very typical of him. "Put on your leather jacket," he said in that paternal, authoritative tone I knew so well. I protested half-heartedly: "But dad, this is a dress for such an occasion..." And then, with a wink, he explained: "It's so cold today, I don't want you to get cold!" But I knew full well that it wasn't about the cold. That was just his charming excuse, his humorous attempt to wrap it up nicely.

The truth was: it was never about the weather. It was about not showing too much of myself—my shoulders, my body. That was important to him. It always had been. No matter where we went, whether to Betzenberg, to a national game, or to an official reception, I often had to change clothes several times before we left the house. "That's too short, that's too see-through," he would say. Although I always dressed rather conservatively, especially when I was out with him, it was never enough. I knew it, I accepted it, and although inwardly I sometimes rolled my eyes, I understood: it was his way of protecting me. So, with a sigh, I pulled my leather jacket over my fancy dress and walked down the red carpet next to my father like a rebellious girl. It was as if I were 16 again, as if I were little Dagmar again, whom daddy always had to keep an eye on. Even though I grumbled to myself, I knew: this was love. This was care. This was my father.

The red carpet was full of glitz and glamour. Reporters flashed their cameras, people called out names, celebrities smiled for the cameras. But for me, none of that mattered. For me, the most important person that evening was the man beside me, walking with me step by step, hand in hand, across the red ribbon of history.

It was a very special experience for me to sit next to my father in the theater and see a young actor portraying him on the stage. My father was part of a historic event that was made into a film half a century later. That was simply incredible to me. My father was excited too. The lights dimmed, the curtain rose—and then it began. "The Miracle of Bern" came to life. I felt goosebumps crawl up my spine as I heard the first bars of music, and my father's story was brought to life by the actors on stage. The names, the voices, the scenes—suddenly they were all back. It was as if someone had turned back time, as if I were seeing my father once again as a young man, part of that legendary team that made history.

The scene where the actors reenacted the soccer game was particularly breathtaking—not with a real ball or on grass, but as an elaborate piece of choreography on the wall, using silhouettes, creating living sculptures. I held my breath. So did my father next to me. It felt like the past and present were connecting, as if the stage had become a screen for his memories. I glanced at him. His eyes were bright, and his hands rested quietly on the armrests, as if he wanted to hold onto the moment. I placed my hand on his, and he squeezed it lightly. No words were needed, just a quiet, understanding nod. We both knew this wasn't just a performance. It was a deep dive into a story that meant everything to him and, for me, a reminder of a father who was so much more than just a world champion.

The premiere after-party was in full swing. Champagne glasses clinked, laughter filled the air, and well-wishes were exchanged. But for both of us, the evening was more than just a celebration. It was a quiet victory, a tribute to our journey together over the years, and an evening that reminded me just how much love and devotion were in my father's actions. Even though I walked the red carpet in a leather jacket, I would do it again in a heartbeat, because to me, it will always mean: I am daddy's girl. And this daddy, this man from another era, always protected me.

"Wetten, dass..?"—An evening full of laughter, pride, and a touch of madness

In October 2014, my father and I traveled to Erfurt to attend the legendary ZDF show "Wetten, dass...?" To him, it wasn't just a regular night of television. It was a celebration, a trip down memory lane, a moment of glory in the spotlight. To me, it was much more. It was a trip with my father, where I wasn't just his daughter, but his devoted companion, making sure everything went smoothly. My father was over 80 at the time. But anyone who knew Horst Eckel knew that he commented on his age with a playful grin and a twinkle in his eyes. Even before the trip, he had told me in that unique tone only he could manage, making every request sound both affectionate and firm: "Sweetheart, I want to climb as few stairs as possible. And you make sure I don't overdo it."

I nodded dutifully. "Of course, dad, I'll take care of everything." After all, we had just completed a long flight, and I wanted his appearance to be as effortless as possible. When we entered the studio, the atmosphere was electric. Cameramen, producers, and technicians with headsets were darting around, lights were flashing, and the audience was buzzing with anticipation. My heart was pounding; my palms were slightly sweaty with nervousness. My father, on the other hand, sat relaxed backstage and watched the commotion with a smile. Only once, as the final preparations were underway, did he quietly say, more to himself than to me, "I hope everything goes smoothly. I don't want to embarrass myself here."

The moment that would throw my careful planning into disarray was not long in coming. A production staff member approached me with a practiced smile and said, "So, we would like Mr. Eckel to come down the grand staircase like all the other guests." He was then to join Benedikt Höwedes, who was also invited and had become world champion with the national team a few months earlier. I stared at the employee as if he had just announced that my father was to jump into the studio on a trampoline. "That's not possible! He's over 80! We discussed this specifically, no big stairs for him!"

"Oh, really? Well, then we'll change it." I breathed a sigh of relief. Everything was sorted. My father would be able to enter the studio relaxed, without having to climb the big staircase. But when I told him about it, he winked at me with his famous smile and the little, cheeky twinkle in his eyes that only he could do, and said quietly, with that loving, mischievous undertone: "Why can't I go down the big stairs? If the others can do it, so can I!" I sighed. "Dad, I reorganized everything especially to make it easier for you!"

"Oh, nonsense," he said with a grin. "What they can do, I can do too. I can still do it!"

So the whole thing had to be undone. The grand staircase, however, stayed. The moment arrived and the studio audience was buzzing with anticipation. I sat next to Sönke Wortmann, the director of the film "The Miracle of Bern", and my heart was pounding. My hands were sweaty, and I had butterflies in my stomach. "Please, please, let him get down those stairs safely," I prayed silently. And then he appeared. My father. Proud, straight-backed, with a confident walk, as if he'd always been a star. The audience couldn't hold back any longer. As he descended the grand staircase, the crowd rose to its feet. A standing ovation for the last hero of Bern. The applause swelled, people clapped and shouted his name, and the whole hall seemed to shake with excitement. Tears welled up in my eyes. My father beamed—not out of arrogance, but touched, humble, just as he always was.

Sitting right beside Megan Fox and her co-star Will Arnett on the famous couch, he certainly enjoyed the company of such a beautiful woman. Perhaps he even indulged in a little of his characteristic, charming, old-fashioned flirting. Yet, we both understood—and he knew it most clearly—that his heart belonged to only one woman: my mother. The playful exchange was nothing more than a small, affectionate jest, a silent wink that communicated, "I'm having fun and enjoying this moment, but my true love waits at home."

While my father was clearly at ease, I sat somewhat anxiously in the front row of the audience during the show. The show progressed, and we had originally agreed that he would return to the audience after his interview so he could rest. But when he was politely asked to do so, he leaned back, relaxed, tilted his head slightly, and said with a small grin and that typical dry calm: "Why? I'm quite comfortable here." And so he stayed for the entire show. Chatting, laughing, as if he had always belonged to this glittering world of television.

After the show, we drove back to the hotel. I was exhausted; it had been a long day, and my feet were aching. Well, I thought, dad isn't a spring chicken anymore, so we'll probably just have a quick nightcap at the bar. But I hadn't accounted for his charisma. He settled in at the hotel bar, ordered a drink, then another, striking up conversations with anyone who didn't manage to look away fast enough. He laughed and talked as if it were the best night of his life. I sat next to him, barely awake, while my father held court at the hotel bar. When I checked my watch, it was almost 3 AM. The boys from pop group Tokio Hotel had been asleep for hours, but my father was still going strong—beaming, full of energy.

"Dad, we have to go upstairs now," I finally said, a little pleadingly. "It's really late, and you should lie down now, okay?" He just grinned at me, raised his glass, winked at me with his mischievous eyes, and said, "Oh, come on, life is short. Let's stay a little longer." When we finally made it to our respective rooms sometime in the early hours of the morning, I fell into bed, exhausted. But who was standing at my door the next morning, bright and early at seven, fresh as the morning dew? My dad. "Honey, come on, we have to eat breakfast! It's already late!" he called. I dragged myself to the restaurant like a zombie, while he cheerfully sipped his coffee, read the newspaper, and greeted the bartender from the night before with a hearty "Good morning!" Right then and there, I realized once again that this was typical of my father. Indestructible, full of humor, full of life, and with a little smile on his face because he knew he was still the charming guy who made everyone laugh. What more could you want?

Sunday stories from the jungle

There are Sunday stories, and then there is our Sunday story. Not just any story. Not one you find in picture books. Not one that begins with "Once upon a time ..." either. Ours begins quietly, with a three-year-old girl tiptoeing down the hallway in her pajamas, on her tiptoes so that her mom wouldn't hear her. Her mom had already gotten up and was busy somewhere with an ironing board or preparing bread rolls. But her dad was still asleep. And that was my chance.

I carefully pushed open the door, like a little secret agent. It creaked. I held my breath. No reaction. Good. Mission Cuddle Adventure could begin. I crept into dad's bed, crawled under the covers, right next to him. He blinked. Just one eye. Then the other. And finally, a grin that said "Aha, it's you again!"

"Hey there, do you want to hear a story?"

THAT was the sentence. The magic key to the best stories I'd ever heard in my life. We pulled the blanket over our heads. Our secret tent. Our pillow cave. Our own world, where only the two of us existed, along with a few hundred dangerous natives, an airplane, a jungle, and a cauldron full of hot water.

"So, listen..." dad started, his voice deep and quiet, as if it had swallowed a bit of jungle smoke. "My crew and I were flying on an airplane—a really big one—heading for America. Everything was going smoothly. We were eating cookies, drinking soda, and I was dozing off a little when suddenly..."

BOOM!

"A bang! As if someone had hit the landing gear with a baseball bat!

The whole plane started to shake. The seats shook, the coffee spilled over—and then... we went down."

I pulled the blanket tighter around me. Dad was now making these little hand movements, as if he were shaking his invisible plane. "We were going down. Very fast. But not like when you land, more like a crazy carousel spinning too fast. Everyone was pale, some were screaming. But all I could think about was telling you about it later."

"Then BOOM! We landed. Not at an airport. No, in the middle of the jungle. In the middle of trees. Mud. Vines. The wings of the plane hung in the trees like wet shirts." I imagined it vividly: a plane in the jungle, with a banana on the cockpit and dad's scarf hanging out the window. "We crawled out of the wreckage. At first we were all very quiet. Only jungly sounds around us, screeching, rustling, humming. The jungle is alive. Very!"

"And then?" I asked breathlessly.

"Then we had to leave. On foot. Through the mud. With our suitcases. One of us still had his cleats on. He immediately got stuck like a garden gnome in a flower bed."

"We walked for three days and ate fruit. Some of it was sweet, some bitter. One guy bit into a purple fruit, and afterwards his tongue was blue and he could only whistle instead of speak. I didn't eat anything. As you know, I was always the skinny Tarzan of the group. Just skin and bones. But fast as the wind." I nodded. Of course dad was fast. The fastest. Obviously.

"But on the third day, we realized we weren't alone. There was whispering. Rustling. Eyes in the thicket. Shadows moved only when we didn't." I got goosebumps. Dad did too. I could tell. "And then, BAM! They were there. Masks, drums, spears, painted faces. It happened so fast. They came from all directions. Pfffft! A blowpipe! Zap—one of us was hit and just dropped like a sack of potatoes."

"We were tied up, dragged away, and carried into the village like sacks of potatoes. They were talking wildly, a language like: 'Dschupadschapa-Mahamba-Woosh!' I didn't understand a word, but I knew it was serious." I giggled. Dad always made the chief's voice particularly high-pitched and loud. "They paraded us around. Then they locked us up. Three of us in a bamboo hut with no windows. But, clever as we were, we carved a hole in the wall so we could spy."

"And then...?" I whispered.

"Then we saw it. They took the first of us. Right in the center of the village stood a huge, steaming cauldron. They threw in herbs. And him." I gasped. Every single time. Even the twelfth time. "And it kept happening. Every day, one of us disappeared. By the last day, I was the only one left. They came and got me, too. They put me in the cauldron. Luckily, the water was still cold." Dad then did that funny voice he always used when he shivered.

"I just sat there for a moment. Then I thought, I have to find a way out of here. That's when I realized the cauldron had a round bottom, like an old rocking horse. I started to rock it. Just a little at first. Then more. Faster and faster! Right – left – SPLASH! I tipped it over! The water spilled out with me. I slid down the embankment like I was on a soapy slide! And I ran and ran! They were chasing me with spears, drums, and shouts, but they didn't stand a chance. I was too fast for them!"

"I made it to another village. The people were friendly. They gave me clothes, a radio—and then a plane arrived. I was rescued."

I breathed a sigh of relief. Every time.

Years later, when I was maybe five or six, I finally dared to ask. "Dad... but... how can that be? I know the others. They're all still alive... weren't they eaten?" Dad looked at me. He blinked. And then he grinned.

"Aren't you a clever little girl? Just like your dad."

And we pulled the blanket back over our heads in our cave, where cannibals live, jungle birds screech, and a grinning father is the best storyteller in the world.

Between worlds: The quiet path to my father

My father was present—and he wasn't emotionally distant. I always felt his tenderness, closeness, and reliability. He held my hand, put his arm around me; I often sat on his lap. I felt warmth, security, and connection. His love was quiet, but undeniable. And yet, there was something he couldn't express, precisely when words were needed most. When it came to feelings, conflicts, or anything that caused pain, he would withdraw. He couldn't talk about it, not because he didn't want to, but because he had never learned how.

No one had taught him how to open up through language during his childhood, so he avoided it. Silence was his shield, sometimes lasting for days, even weeks. Three or four weeks without a single word. That's difficult for a child to understand. No arguments, no explanations—just distance. And with that came the quiet question: Do I still matter? Did I do something wrong? It took me years to realize: It wasn't rejection; it was his own deep insecurity. His silence was his clumsy attempt to avoid hurting anyone—and yet, that's exactly what it did.

I promised myself I would be different. I am a different person. I'm impulsive, direct, and sometimes loud. I say what I think—perhaps too quickly sometimes, but never with malice. I argue, yes, but I also forgive quickly. And I speak up. I'm convinced that vulnerability is the only path to genuine closeness. It's the only way to truly connect.

My mother was strong, demanding, and unshakeable. She often said, "I need you like the air I breathe. You're the only one who does everything the way I do." I became a confidante at an early age. A co-responsible person. A little adult. In my childhood, I was often the one who reconciled the two sides. When there was trouble, I mediated, not out of duty, but because I felt that otherwise everything would fall apart. I stepped back when necessary. I was often overlooked, but I didn't care. I didn't need a stage. I needed harmony, especially with my father.

I watched how often he felt out of place—like a guest in his own home. He was pushed to the sidelines, and I knew he wanted to belong, but there was nothing I could do to change that. The real turning point came in 1985, when I was seventeen. That wonderful, confusing age when you don't know much about the world yet, but your heart sometimes feels like it's about to burst. Everything feels a little too immediate, too overwhelming, too intense, too mysterious. You don't know exactly what you're looking for, but you can feel that something is missing.

A counterpart. A glance.

A quiet: "I see you."

My mother was always there. She was loving, present, and warm. But I felt like I was missing something else: the male perspective. A father who shared his point of view, who listened in his own way, who was present when it truly mattered. As was so often the case, my father was rarely home. Not because he didn't want to be, but because he was a famous man, constantly traveling and on the road. I never had a clear father figure. I missed him, perhaps more than I realized at the time.

But there was a bond between us. My mother once said that the moment he picked me up for the first time—so very carefully—everything became clear. There was something palpable between us, like a quiet force. Over time, though, that bond became less visible because he was away so often, because we didn't talk, and because I never really knew him. Then, as a teenager, you start asking yourself those silent questions you don't voice aloud: Would he have preferred a son? Would he understand me if I told him my thoughts? Am I even like him? I didn't know. Until that summer.

As a child, I wasn't really aware that I was missing a father figure. I always watched "Little House on the Prairie" and thought Charles Ingalls was a great father. Sometimes I wished I had that kind of relationship, but I had my mother, who was my rock. At least back then, I thought she was enough. But here and now, I realized I needed something else—the male perspective, a different view of life. I knew I would find it.

And I did. I got in the car with him—just like that—and insisted on going with him to the 1. FC Kaiserslautern games. I knew soccer was an important part of his life. If I really wanted to get to know him, I had to be there with him. At first, it was unusual for him to take someone along. But I stuck with it. Eventually, it became a normal thing. Later, he said, "I won't go without you." I went with him, first as his daughter and later as his manager. To large public events, red carpets, award ceremonies—we stood side by side. He'd take me in his arms and never overshadow me. He spoke about me. About us. He'd say, "Without my wife, without my family, I wouldn't be the man I am today." He said it publicly, and he meant it. I'll never forget that. At first, he was my shield, but at some point, very quietly, I became his.

It touched me deeply because I realized the time would come when he would no longer be with us. And that I would then carry on his legacy alone—a silent legacy of love. I accepted it with pride. My mother also had her own way of loving. She was present, unwavering, and clear. She held us close, perhaps sometimes too tightly. But she was there for us when no one else was. Both loved in their own way, and I understood them both.

I remember a scene where I hadn't put my clothes away properly. My mother flew into a rage, tearing everything out of the closet and chasing me through the house. My father stepped between us, clear and determined for the first time. "Stop it. She's not a child anymore. If you keep this up, we'll lose her." Eventually, I moved out. Not in anger, but in peace. It was time for my freedom, for her space, and for a new balance between us.

Today, there is no bitterness. Only love. Even though both my parents are no longer here, I miss them every day. But they left something behind that remains: the ability to forgive, to understand, and to love. And the strength to move on—with dignity, with pride, with joy in my heart.

And above all: with love.

Riptide

It was Thursday, June 27, 1985, 5:50 PM. It was the beginning of something special. Something that would connect me to my father for all time. I happened to see the series "Riptide," or, as it was called in our country, "Trio with Four Fists." Three men, a boat, a pink helicopter. Action, humor, sun, friendship, but above all, ethos.

There was Cody, the charming daredevil. Murray, the gentle, clever tinkerer with a heart of gold, and Nick Ryder. Tall. Dark-haired. Well built. And those blue eyes—clear, alert, a little lost. He was cool, courageous, and direct, but never arrogant. He had a sense of humor, a rebellious side, but also depth. A hard shell and a soft core. He didn't talk much, but when he spoke, he was honest. Something about him touched me deeply. I felt a connection without knowing exactly why. Perhaps because he had traits that I didn't know or couldn't see in my father, perhaps because he embodied something that I lacked, or perhaps because I saw the person behind the façade.

I watched the first episodes alone. A silent ritual. Just me and my three heroes. And then came this one evening. I was sitting on the sofa with my legs tucked under me, the intro was playing—and suddenly my father came in. Very calm. Completely at ease. He said nothing, sat down, and stayed until the end. I felt that he was watching me, but I pretended not to notice. After the credits rolled, he only said: "I like this show."

A week later, he was already sitting there when I entered the room with a glass of beer, a sandwich, and a twinkle in his eye. Then he said: "Well, what took you so long? Your Nick is about to save the world again!" My Nick? I blushed and laughed. Of course, I was a bit annoyed. But I knew that it was his way of being close to me. It was affection, genuine interest, a small, silent token of love. At that moment, I realized that he saw me. He understood me.

From then on, we watched every episode together. And very slowly something began to grow. We talked and laughed. We talked about Cody,

Murray, and Nick, but then we also talked about friendship, soccer, camaraderie, and justice. I listened and learned so much more about my father. His values, his attitude toward life—I saw him properly for the first time. We were alike, more alike than I had ever dared hope. He listened to me, and for the first time in my life, I was sure. I had a father who loved me again.

The three men on the screen allowed us to connect. They gave us language, closeness, togetherness. It was a ritual that connected us. Whenever we couldn't watch an episode of the series at home, we recorded it on video. Next to soccer, this was our second bridge to each other. I am grateful for the series to this day, because it brought my father back to me. It was the turning point in our relationship. I soon accompanied him everywhere. To sporting events, to receptions, to the stadium. He became my shield, and over time, as he got older, I quietly became his. Many years later, he would entrust me with everything: His legacy. His story. His voice. It all started on that Thursday evening with three heroes on the screen and a hero right next to me.

Today, many years later, I'm standing in America—in Los Angeles, in Philadelphia, or in St. Louis—and maybe someday these three men will read my words: Joe Penny. Perry King. Thom Bray.

They don't know it, but they set something in motion, all those years ago. They supported a girl who didn't know how to allow closeness. And a father who wanted to learn how closeness works. Without knowing it, they built a bridge between two people who had been unable to find each other for a long time. And I am grateful for that from the bottom of my heart.

If I ever met them, I might blush, I might stammer, I might smile like the girl I was back then, but I would tell them: You gave me back my father. Thank you. Not with big words. Not with great deeds, but with something much greater: Closeness! One moment. One series. One connection.

If my father had ever met them, he would have slapped them on the shoulder and said to them: "Hey, so you're the three Riptide guys. Smart, cool, handsome... I always thought our soccer team was turbulent, but compared to you guys, it was almost peaceful on the field." And his light blue eyes would have sparkled with mischief. Then he would have sat down with them—quietly, naturally, as if it were completely normal—and said: "I think I could have kept up with you. You were a good team, real friends. I liked your attitude. Keep it up!"

These three men flickered not only across the screen, but directly into my heart. If I could meet them one day, it would be a brief moment of eternity for me, being seventeen again, hearing my mother and grandmother's voices in the kitchen, sitting on the sofa next to my father, just him and me, for the last time.

To my Riptide heroes:

"Meeting you would be the greatest gift I could receive. One last moment with my father."

(Dedicated with gratitude to Joe Penny, Perry King, and Tom Bray)

For my mother

About nine months after my father passed away, in late summer 2022, I had to make a tough call: some of his estate needed to be sold. This decision was driven by two factors: my mother's significantly worsening health and care needs, and the increasing safety concerns around the house in Vogelbach where the estate was stored. My worries about security were sadly confirmed by an attempted break-in at the Horst Eckel House in Kusel.

The sale's sole purpose was to secure my mother's long-term care. It was extremely important to me that the memorabilia went to worthy hands—genuine soccer fans and collectors, not just people looking for a trophy. Selling them on the black market was unthinkable. That's why I approached Wolfgang Fuhr of Agon Sportsworld GmbH, a well-known auction house for sports memorabilia.

This was an incredibly difficult decision, despite the careful thought I put into it. My father had dedicated his life to soccer, and every piece of memorabilia reminded me of him. But I knew this was the only way to give my mother the retirement she deserved.

Six weeks before the auction, I held a press conference. I knew my decision would provoke criticism. Journalists asked if there was truly no other alternative. I explained that I had reached out to both 1. FC Kaiserslautern and the German Soccer Association (DFB) in an effort to keep the collection together, but had been unsuccessful. Both organizations were invited to the press conference but did not attend.

The Sepp Herberger Foundation, whose charter is to support "members of the soccer community in need," was also mentioned. I had described my mother's situation to them, but assistance would only have been possible if we had disclosed all our financial information—including the sale of a house. That was simply out of the question for us. "We are not in need," I told the journalists. "My father was a proud man, and my mother is a proud woman. She would never ask for anything we could handle ourselves." I also made it clear that personal items, such as letters, the wristwatch from the 1954 World Cup, and my father's love letters to my mother—"matters of the heart"—would stay within the family. I would have preferred a reputable institution to acquire the entire estate. But since no such buyer could be found, the auction had to take place in November 2022.

A journalist recently recalled a 2019 statement my father made about never wanting to part with his memorabilia. I was there for the conversation—it wasn't an official statement, just a casual exchange during an exhibition. "The world was a different place back then," I responded. "My parents never expected to need full-time care. Unfortunately, things turned out differently, and at some point, it became clear we'd face significant, unexpected costs."

To this day, I hope that soccer fans understand my decision. I explained my reasons objectively and with complete transparency, including the fact that my father himself would have made the same choice. "Objects are objects, and people are people" was one of his favorite quotes. Even though every piece was dear to my heart, one thing was clear: people come first. The press conference was followed by individual interviews after Wolfgang Fuhr presented some of the auction items, including the blank player ID card from the 1954 World Cup, the winner's medal, his soccer shoes, and a photo of the final's jersey. This jersey, along with the shorts and socks, was the highlight of the auction—a complete kit that my father had worn several times during the World Cup.

Fuhr emphasized the authenticity of all the items, each of which was individually certified. He explained that the jerseys were used several times back then because the players didn't swap them out after the game as they do today. I was especially proud that my father had kept and preserved these items himself for years for future generations, including the jersey he wore in the 1954 World Cup final—along with the shorts and socks—in our home. It was important to him to keep these mementos in the family. It was only many years later, at the opening of the German Soccer Museum, that he loaned them to the museum. It was always understood that these items would remain the property of our family. After my father's death, they legally passed to my mother, his sole heir.

I had already spoken candidly with my father about this topic during his lifetime. I wanted to know how he would feel if I were forced to part with some of his memorabilia one day. He looked at me, put his hand on my shoulder, and said something I will never forget: "All these things are mementos, yes—but things are just things. It's people that matter. And I would do anything for your mother. And for you." That gave me the strength to move forward. I had reclaimed the jersey in time. Although it was still in the museum at the time of the press conference because the loan agreement had not yet expired, the ownership was clearly established. The auction was completely legally sound, and it was also justified on a human level. My father hadn't kept these items for the museum; he kept them for us.

The auction took place a few weeks later. I did not participate. The proceeds ensured my mother's long-term care. The loss was painful, but necessary. I was convinced that my father would have supported this decision. So I am delighted that it is now on display at the DFB Museum in Dortmund, because this is exactly what we all wanted: it will all be preserved for future generations, and the legend of Bern lives on, and with it, my father.

Looking back, the decision was painful but correct. The high esteem in which my father was held at the auction touched me deeply. I still feel connected to him today and know that I acted in his spirit. "I hope," I said at the end of the press conference, "that everyone who bought a piece at the auction will treat it with the respect that the heroes of 1954 deserve. If that happens, I can find peace with this decision."

I faced the accusations, the hostility, the hurtful insinuations, and even the anonymous death threats that were made against me because of the auction. But I endured it all because I knew why I had done it. Not out of self-interest. Not to make a profit, but to keep my promise—the promise to be there for my parents when they needed me.

I did it because my father loved my mother more than anything. And I know that he would have supported this decision. No matter what the public thinks or says about me.

I did it out of love. For my mother.

The Second Whistle—Breaking New Ground

When I reflect on the years my father spent in Völklingen, I can still feel his pride and passion for soccer and for the community he worked and played with there. For him, Völklingen was more than just a brief stop after 1. FC Kaiserslautern; it was a new chapter at a time when he was uncertain about his future.

In 1960, he transferred to SV Röchling Völklingen, stepping down from professional soccer to the amateur league. At the time, this meant a one-year suspension. However, instead of retiring or complaining, my father seized the chance to learn something new. He earned his coaching license and dedicated himself wholeheartedly to coaching the club. I remember his stories from that period. He spoke enthusiastically about leading the team to the championship in the Saarland amateur league and securing their direct promotion to the 2nd League Southwest. He wasn't just a coach; he was a true team player, even though he couldn't yet step onto the field.

He was finally allowed to play again starting in 1961. He may have been the "Hero of Bern," but in Völklingen, he was simply "Horst." He didn't want to be the star; he wanted to work hard, honestly, and with discipline alongside his team. He played until 1965, making 57 appearances in the Regional League, and quietly ended his active career without a fuss after an away game against Phönix Bellheim. But that was by no means the end of his time in Völklingen. He remained loyal to the club. He returned as a coach and even guided the team to the round of 16 in the DFB Cup in the 1967/68 season. He often mentioned the victory against Werder Bremen, not to brag, but because he was so incredibly proud of the team. I could sense how much that community meant to him.

In addition to soccer, he worked in administration at the Röchling factory, where he was also in charge of apprentice sports. His later decision to become a teacher was a natural continuation of what had always been important to him: encouraging young people, instilling values, and giving back. As his daughter, I can see today how much those years shaped him. Völklingen was a place of fresh starts, friendship, and authenticity for him. He made an impact there not only as a soccer player but also as a person. I am proud that I got to witness that and that he showed me how to navigate life with character and heart.

From soccer player to teacher with heart

When my father decided to become a teacher, I was only two years old. The decision wasn't made on a sudden whim, but very deliberately, in close consultation with my mother. His own mother also played an important role in this: he once stated clearly that he wouldn't have taken this step if she had been against it. But my mother, who assessed the situation very realistically and wisely, immediately recognized it was a sound decision. And she was right. It was the ideal profession for him—perhaps even his true calling, second only to soccer. The teaching internship was made possible by one of his former soccer teammates, who had since become a minister. Thanks to this connection, my father was given a second chance to become a teacher at the age of 38.

In 1970, we moved to Morbach, where we lived until 1973. It was an intense, exhausting, and formative time. My father worked at the school during the day and coached in the afternoon, while my mother managed our hotel. She didn't just manage it; she pulled it out of debt. Sometimes she stayed up until two in the morning doing the accounts, then got up at five to go to the market for supplies. Later, she even took over the cooking herself. She only had one cleaning lady to help her. Despite the immense pressure, our house was always bustling, and the hotel was constantly booked solid. But as a family, we paid a price for this.

I hardly saw my parents during that time. They worked all day and evening. I remember often sitting on my mother's lap at night—that was our time together. When she finally went to bed, she took me with her. It wasn't much, but it was closeness, warmth, and security. Although I was sometimes lonely back then, that time also strengthened me. I became independent and mature early on, partly because I at least had my grandmother by my side. Unfortunately, my grandfather had already died of a heart attack. My father was a rock amid all the chaos. When he finished his teaching internship and the students found out he would be leaving their school, they suddenly showed up in front of our hotel. A whole crowd of young people shouted loudly: "Eckel! Eckel! Eckel! We want Mr. Eckel back!"

It was a moment that still shows me today what kind of teacher he was. For him, teaching was never just about the subject matter or merely a duty—it was always about the people. He was strict, yes, but always fair. He treated his students with respect without ever demand ing respect in return. And that's exactly what they sensed. That's exactly what they valued. Today, I am grateful for what I experienced as a child. It wasn't always easy, but I learned what responsibility means, what solidarity means, what it takes to not just get by, but to truly build something. My parents exemplified this for me every single day.

Childhood between the nine-pin bowling alley and the classroom

During this time, I was supposed to go to kindergarten, but I didn't particularly enjoy it. Mostly because my mother was never able to pick me up on time. I often had to wait a long time for her, sometimes over an hour. I would sit quietly on the bench, swinging my legs, waiting. My mother always said later that I had been very well-behaved. There was no other choice, and I understood that somehow.

But sometimes there were little adventures: Once, my mother was very late picking me up. The kindergarten teacher didn't know what to do with me, so she simply took me to the bakery. I got a piece of cake—what a treat! But my mother didn't know that. When she came to pick me up, I had disappeared. Panic set in. She immediately called my father at school, who had the class interrupted. Teachers, students—everyone was looking for me. Then they found me happily nibbling on my cake, completely unaware of the commotion. It was less happy for the kindergarten teacher, because she got into trouble, of course.

Another time, I was bored at kindergarten again. I knew where my dad worked, so I just set off. In my slippers, I trudged to the school, searched through the building, and finally found him in the conference room. I threw open the door, stood with my legs apart, and said loudly, "I'm looking for my dad!" He looked up, laughed, and picked me up. I was allowed to spend the rest of the conference there—my personal throne.

I was always on the go anyway. When I ran away, I was often brought back by the mail carrier or the garbage collector. Everyone knew me. "Oh, the little girl from the Eckel Hotel," they said, smiling, and passed me on like a little town secret. I was always looking for adventure, everywhere. When I was at the hotel, I came up with my own ways to earn a little pocket money. I stood at the entrance, waited for new guests to arrive, and politely offered to carry their bags. Sometimes a suitcase, sometimes a coat. Of course, they gave me spare change for it—a few pennies, sometimes more. Everything went into my piggy bank. I was very proud of my little business model. My little entrepreneurial heart blossomed until my mother found out. That was the end of my entrepreneurship—she didn't find it as charming as I did.

I also learned English early on. We had many English and American guests, and I wasn't shy. My mother often told me how I would go up to one of the guests, put my hands on my hips, and confidently say, "How do you do? My name is Dagmar."

We also had our own nine-pin bowling alley in the house, which became the stage for our games. Our favorite game was "Star Trek." I was Captain Kirk, of course. Once, while watching the pins being pulled up, I got stuck myself. I was lifted up with them—a real space adventure with an emergency landing. Captain Kirk had the day off from flying that day.

During this time, my father taught me how to ride a bike in his own unique way. He simply put me on the bike, pushed me along, and shouted, "I'm holding you!" But he only did that for the first few feet. Then he let go, and I rode. Just like that. I remember how surprised I was, but also how proud. There was a hayloft in the old barn behind the house, and we were allowed to jump into the hay. It was paradise for children. I loved it. But not everything was completely safe.

When I learned to swim and ski

I was two and a half years old when I learned to swim. Not in the usual way. No brightly colored flotation devices or games that suggested the water was just a fun playground. No. My swimming lessons were a mix of fatherly love, a deep desire to save lives, and—let's be honest—a bit of clever strategy, because my father always had a plan. He rarely talked about his emotions, but I knew something had profoundly affected him. Before I was even born, he had pulled two children out of the water at the outdoor pool below our hotel. He was only able to save one. He didn't speak about the other child very often, but when he did, his voice would drop, and his eyes would suddenly reveal something that I, as a child, couldn't name, only sense. Sadness. Maybe guilt, too. But definitely an unwavering determination.

"Before I ever have to pull you out of there," he said quietly, "I'll teach you." So there I stood. Two and a half years old. Tiny. Wearing water wings that looked like they were made for adult elephants. I had skinny legs, blonde braids, and a swimsuit covered in frogs. I was ready, or at least I thought I was. My father stood at the edge of the pool with his arms crossed and a serious look on his face. No entertainment, no playful dolphin, no foam mat. Just him, the pool, and me. "Alright," he said, "let's go, my little pool bug." At first, he let me splash around. I kicked my legs in the shallow end, squealed, laughed, and felt proud. But my father had been subtly manipulating the water wings. Every day, he'd let a tiny bit of air out of them. Not enough to notice immediately, just enough that I had to paddle a little harder the next day to stay afloat. "Dad, they're broken," I said at one point.

"No, no—they're training with you," he said, grinning. And so it went, day after day. Less air, more confidence. And then came that one moment.

I was back in the water, the wings nearly flat. I was paddling, and I suddenly felt that they were no longer supporting me. I gasped for air, but I didn't sink. I was swimming. All by myself. Without help. Without even knowing how. I turned around, my face dripping wet, my eyes huge. "Dad! I can do it!" He didn't say anything. But he smiled. A genuine smile. Not the polite one he gave the hotel guests. The one only I knew. "I knew it." Then he stretched out his arms, lifted me out of the pool, and hugged me as if I had just won a championship. And to him, I had. His little champion.

From then on, water was my second home. I jumped off the edge of the pool, dove from the three-meter board, retrieved rings, and floated backward on air mattresses. I was free and fearless. But I was still myself. The child who constantly disappeared. Once, half the hotel staff was looking for me. In the bathroom. In the changing rooms. Even in the trash cans. "Where is Dagmar?!" The answer came from the lifeguard. I was sitting next to him, dangling my feet, happier than ever. In front of me: a large slice of crumb cake. "I was hungry," was all I said. "And besides, it was so nice and quiet here." My father rolled his eyes, my mother sighed, but I knew: I was back and I could swim.

Skiing wasn't a leisure activity for us; it was practically an educational mission. My father, the strong-willed champion, wanted to teach me how to glide through the snow on two boards. I was maybe four or five years old, small, determined, and bundled up warmly. What I didn't have: appropriate skis. What I got instead: two giant slats that looked more like fence posts. I looked like a girl mounted on two broomsticks. But my father was not to be deterred. "You are going to learn this now," he said. I nodded. He showed me how to keep my balance—briefly, clearly, practically. Then he placed me on a snowy meadow behind the hotel and gave me a little push. "Now go." And I went. Straight ahead. Without stopping. Without turning.

Right across the flower bed that was actually being prepared for spring.

I flattened everything: tulip bulbs, freshly planted onions, little sticks with flower names on them—everything was flat. In the end, I landed in a bush. My skis were stuck, and I laughed. My dad didn't laugh right away. But then he said dryly, "All right. You slowed down. Not graceful, but effectively." The flower bed was ruined. I was proud. My mother looked at the battlefield and simply said, "At least now we have room for new ideas." I learned to ski that day. Elegance came later. Maybe.

Sledding noise and garage ban

I was four years old—old enough to know speed was fun, and young enough to ignore the consequences. Snow was falling, the slope was white, and my sled was ready. It wasn't small. It was solid, heavy, and made of wood, with a seat board perfect for a brave kid who had little sense of braking. I climbed aboard. My mother had warned me to be careful. My father was standing somewhere off to the side. I remember the wind in my face, the crunch of snow under the runners, and the feeling: the faster, the better!

Unfortunately, the slope wasn't empty. Unfortunately, someone was in the way. An older girl, an acquaintance, as I later found out. I saw her too late, or maybe not at all. Before anyone could react, my sled hit her head-on. She fell, screamed, and stayed on the ground. I kept going, like a mini-torpedo, until I flipped over myself. Then it got quiet. Only the girl's crying echoed across the meadow. She ended up in the hospital with a broken leg. I had a few scratches, but I was in shock, which was worse than anything else. I didn't understand what had happened, only that I had done something wrong—that someone was suffering because of me.

The sled was immediately taken to the garage. My father said nothing. My mother just said, "That's it for sledding for now." I understood. I was sorry. And yet I knew: I wasn't bad, just brave. Too brave, perhaps. A little girl with a sled that was too big and a heart that was too fast. And with parents who, despite everything, didn't scold, but explained.

Three meters above the marble

My sister and I were incredibly bored one day at the hotel. She was nine years old, a little bossy, but also my hero because she was so tall and confident.

I followed her everywhere—unfortunately, that included ideas that sounded great in theory but were terrible in practice. We were standing on the hotel balcony. Three meters below us was the hard marble floor of the entrance area. No grass, no flower beds—just solid marble, as hard as could be. My sister held my doll over the railing. I don't recall exactly why. Maybe we were playing that the doll could fly. Maybe it was a game of cowboys and Indians, or some dramatic scene. The doll flew. But not for long. It fell with full force onto the stone-hard marble.

I didn't scream—I just stared. The doll's head shattered, its arms detached from its legs. A toy massacre. But what happened next was much worse: I suddenly felt her hands under my arms. My sister was now holding me over the railing—upside down, a mixture of a game and a dare. To her, it was a joke. For me, it was a moment of sheer terror that seemed to last for minutes. And then my mother appeared in the doorway. She had seen everything: the open balcony door, my dangling legs, the marble floor below. But she didn't scream. No "What are you doing?!" No fit of rage. Just a calm, "Stay calm... don't let go... pull her back up... slowly."

And my sister did it. She pulled me back, trembling. I was on solid ground again. The doll was dead. But I was fine. And my mother left without another word. Later, she simply said, "I didn't scream because I knew she would drop you out of fright." It wasn't just a game anymore. It was a realization: sometimes parents are superheroes, but they're quieter than you'd expect.

Playing with the rope

Sometimes, when adults say, “Kids will be kids,” they don’t realize just how wild children’s imaginations can be. My sister and I often played cowboys and Indians. I was always the Indian, of course. Always. She was the cowboy. Also always. As was common at the time, “arresting” and “tying up prisoners” were part of the game. Only my sister had the brilliant idea to make it seem particularly real. She found a rope—I still don’t know where she got it from—and tied it around my neck. She attached the other end to a doorknob. “You’re my prisoner now. And don’t you dare run away!” Sounds harmless? It wasn’t, because then someone came through the door, opening it. The door swung open, and the rope tightened.

I can only vaguely remember feeling dizzy. My face suddenly felt very hot. I grabbed my neck. I couldn’t say anything, only hope. Luckily, our mother came into the room at that very moment. She saw me, saw the door, the rope, my sister with wide eyes, and reacted immediately. She quickly untied me, without panicking. Then she just sat down next to me and said, “That’s not how you play.” And with that, the game was over.

My sister hadn’t meant any harm. She was completely terrified herself. I was safe again, with a slight blue mark on my neck—a silent reminder of too much imagination and too little knowledge about knots. From that day on, the rule was: No ropes. No neck. No more cowboys. But I remained an Indian nonetheless—proud, defiant, and alive.

The way back to Vogelbach

During my three years in Morbach, I had not only gotten older, but I had also matured. Not in height, but in experience. I knew every nook and cranny around the hotel—every shortcut, every meadow, every shop in town. Not because I just wandered around, but because our guests took me with them. They'd go on trips to the Hunsrück region, hikes, or city visits, and often someone would call the front desk and ask, "Can little Miss Eckel come along?" My mother almost always said yes, probably because she knew I was often better off with so many unfamiliar acquaintances than left unsupervised in the hotel. That's how I got to know the area like the back of my hand. I was a little tour guide with big eyes and endless curiosity.

Then came the day when my father successfully completed his teacher training. Three years of hard work—with classes, studying, soccer practice, and hotel stress. And he had done it. We packed our belongings and moved back to Vogelbach. It wasn't easy to say goodbye—to the hotel, to the smell of the kitchen, to the familiar whirring of the nine-pin bowling alley, to the stairs, the garden, and the streets. To all the stories tucked away in the walls and hallways. Morbach had become a home to me—full of adventure, laughter, mischief... and warmth.

But the next chapter was waiting in Vogelbach.

My father taught there with renewed vigor. He later even took an additional exam in shop class, a subject he particularly liked because it was practical, tangible, and real. Just like him. He loved this profession. Not because he taught, but because he connected with people. He was never someone who spoke down to others. He was someone who took his students seriously and treated them as equals.

For me, the move was a disruption, but also a fresh start. New friends. New streets. New stories. The time in Morbach became a memory. A bright one. A loud one. One that still warms my heart when I think about it today. And sometimes, when I walk through old hotels now, when I hear a bowling alley in the distance or smell fried potatoes and floor polish, I smile quietly, because I know: somewhere between guests and ghosts, suitcases and slices of cake, lies my beginning.

When we moved back to Vogelbach, I was five years old. I started kindergarten and quickly made friends, but of course with the boys. Even then, it was clear: I was the leader of our little gang, which consisted of five or six wild boys and me. We roamed around the area, discovered every hiding spot, built rope swings in the trees, and swung back and forth like Tarzan. Even though we had a swing set and a slide at home, that was far too boring.

One day, I had the brilliant idea of tying our friend Stephan to the slide. I have no idea what I was thinking, but it sounded like fun. Stephan was a good sport and agreed. But physics had other plans: the slide tipped over, fell into the fir tree, and Stephan was left hanging with the rope and slide in the middle of the branches. My mother had to personally rescue him from the tree. Stephan, the living Christmas tree ornament.

We lay on the neighbors' roofs, spitting cherry pits down, throwing water balloons, acting like little anarchists. Of course, neither the neighbors nor our parents found it funny. The punishment came swiftly. But it was worth it. We felt like a gang of little rebels showing the world how to have fun. Once we played detectives, sneaking after an older girl from the village who was driving a car. Somehow we felt it was our duty to tell her parents, which of course got the poor young woman into trouble. She was furious with us, and I can't blame her. But who knows—maybe we actually prevented something worse from happening?

Carnival was our prime time. We made firecracker rockets, threw them at people, played "ding-dong ditch"—until my mother gave me a serious talking-to: "Dagmar, that woman is as old as your grandmother. Do you want your grandmother to be constantly answering the door because children are ringing the bell?" That hit home. I stopped immediately—a moment that has stayed with me to this day. But of course there were other pranks. We built UFOs and—admittedly—set them alight in the neighbor's yard. (Don't worry, there were no big fireworks, just a little smoke and a lot of excitement.) We collected frogs, put them in the neighbor's fountain, listened to the croaking concert, and enjoyed our mischief. Once I even took a frog to school and put it on the head of the girl in front of me. The screaming was fantastic. My parents were less thrilled.

And yet my father was very special to me. Even though he was often absent and my mother practically raised me on her own, he was the one who carved stilts for me, built bows, and made me feel special. I remember the birthday parties in the Obstück (a small orchard area), up above the railroad tracks, where we could run around and play. My mother worked there, cutting trees and paving paths, while I worked with her and felt like I was conquering the world.

Once, I really wanted to spend the night with friends in that little shed with the iron door in the Obstück. Of course, it was a stupid idea, because we had no lamp, it was pitch dark, and the air was getting thinner and thinner. Luckily, my mother came in time, opened the door, and rescued us from our homemade prison cell. A memory that shows me how thin the line between adventure and disaster can be.

Then came the moment when I transitioned back into my role as a girl. It was Christmas, I was fourteen, and my mother gave me a beautiful coat that I would never have worn before. I stood in front of the mirror, my father behind me. He put his hand on my shoulder and said, "I am completely satisfied with my daughters. I would never have wanted any other children—not even sons."

Full circle

Many years had passed since our family moved back to Vogelbach from Morbach. My father had become a respected teacher, a valued colleague, a quiet hero who never sought the spotlight. To some, he remained the "Hero of Bern." To me, he was simply my father—down-to-earth, genuine, and warm-hearted. And yet, a moment came when everything he was, and everything that endured, converged. In 2019, I decided to organize an event in his honor, the first Horst Eckel Gala. It wasn't meant to be a memorial or a retrospective, but a vibrant celebration of a man who had profoundly impacted so many without ever making a fuss about it.

It was a truly special evening. The hall was packed. Celebrities, former teammates, soccer legends, and the media were all there, but more importantly, so were people from his past. Players from Völklingen, former students from his teaching days, and guests from his time in Morbach. Some hadn't seen him for decades; others arrived with pictures, with stories, and with tears in their eyes. They also came with smiles. They didn't talk about him in rehearsed quotes but through genuine memories. One of his former students quietly shared, "Mr. Eckel was the only teacher I truly wanted to listen to." Another whispered to me at the champagne reception, "He was strict, but fair. And he treated us with respect. One never forgets that." The atmosphere was filled with warmth, respect, and gratitude. It was not a somber commemoration but a spirited celebration—an evening that brought everything full circle.

All the stories I carried within me were suddenly more than just childhood memories. They were part of a bigger narrative. They transformed the name 'Horst Eckel' back into the person he truly was: A man of integrity. A loving father. A dedicated teacher. That evening, sitting there, surrounded by voices from the past, I knew that everything we had lived, everything we had preserved, had mattered. It had made a difference. It had left its mark. And I felt a profound sense of pride in the life I had been able to share with my father.

The circle had been completed, but the story lives on.

Embarrasing, personal, happend

In this chapter, I recount some situations that were extremely embarrassing for me, but which happened and cannot be undone. Today, I can laugh heartily about almost all of them, but when they happened, I was anything, but in the mood to laugh. I would have loved to crawl into a mouse hole, as in this first story, for example.

The Braces Attack

I was thirteen or fourteen—the typical age to feel like an ugly duckling. In my case, I was an ugly duckling with braces that consisted of so many brackets and stainless steel archwires that I could easily have rebuilt the Eiffel Tower. And not to be forgotten are the main characters in my story—small elastic bands stretched between my upper and lower jaws to correct my bite. Sounds great, doesn't it? It motivated me to take my first tentative steps toward making contact with the opposite sex.

I was the only girl at school with braces; none of the other girls had them. Today, it seems to be fairly standard, but back then, I was a prototype at my school, running around with eight rubber bands stretched criss-cross in my mouth. The whole contraption made me look like a spider web come to life on two legs. But hey, I was a real one-of-a-kind. Who needs self-confidence when you're armed with such braces? Sure, I was still flat as a board—and not in a cool, athletic "I just finished a master workout" kind of way, but more in a "Hey, are you sure you're not a boy?" kind of way. That was my look. No breasts, no curves, no self-confidence. And then came this sexy brace, which was anything but cool.

But then it happened—that moment every teenager has had, when you think: Today! Today is the day, from today on everything will change. There was this one boy, let's just call him Nick (because he looked like Nick Ryder from "Riptide," my teenage crush. Sooooooo cute!). He was the boy at school that all the girls had a crush on. We all thought he was cool; we all wanted to talk to him. He was the boy who looked so cool when he played guitar that you almost melted away. He was like a typical quarterback from American teen romcoms, but I was anything but the homecoming queen.

So what did I do? I came along with my braces, which could have broadcast a radio transmission, and dared to talk to him. At the time, I thought that was really brave, and to tell the truth, I still think so today. "Hey, Nick," I said—and it came out as if I had just tried to mangle the word "hi" and replace it with a cough. But who cares, because he smiled! I had impressed him; I felt like I was floating on air. Completely detached from the earth... He started talking, and honestly, he was soooo cute. So there I was, with a mouth full of wire and rubber, listening to him as if he were telling me the secrets of the universe. I had my lips pressed so tightly together that I could have started singing "You're My Heart, You're My Soul" at any moment—and then my non-existent coolness factor would have been gone for good.

But fate had to happen. He told me something funny, and I couldn't help it, I laughed, but not a little shy giggle, but my real, loud laugh, that put too much strain on my rubber bands. PING! The rubbers, which were supposed to correct my bite position, shot out of my mouth, freed from their tension, as if there was no tomorrow. It was as if they broke out of their prison and put on an air show. It felt like I was in a bad slapstick movie. One flew straight onto Nick's nose, another landed in his hair with a perfect spin, as if my braces had their own styling approach. The rest thought to themselves, let's fly straight across his cheek, into his T-shirt, and—I swear—one even landed on his shoe!

Nick stared at me with wide-open eyes. I couldn't blame him. Who wants to be a victim of a braces attack? The poor guy must have felt like he was running into a slow-motion action movie apocalypse of braces and rubber, only without the heroic soundtrack and dramatic showdown. Instead, he fumbled around frantically, trying to fish the rubber out of his nose and hair, and I thought: Oh my God, this can't be happening! Then he said in a pained voice, as if he had eaten something bad and needed to find a bathroom as quickly as possible: "Uh... well, I have to... go now. Uh... class is about to start." Class? I looked around. School was long over. What class? We weren't even in school.

And I just thought: Lord in heaven, help me! Where is the hole I can disappear into? Nick, on the other hand, disappeared faster than you could say "school's out." And I stood there, in the midst of my embarrassing existence, my face suddenly turning bright red, and asking myself: "Okay, which city should I move to, or better yet, where do I emigrate to? Bye-bye, dream boy." But it wasn't over yet, because he came back. He handed me the rescued rubber bands and smiled charmingly, saying: "Maybe you can still use them."

Boom, new low!!! The knockout was imminent. I took the rubber bands and, slightly mentally deranged, put them back into my braces. Why????? I screamed inside, but my mind was somewhere in outer space at that moment, unable to align my mind and body. In spite of everything, this was the sweetest and most romantic moment of my life up to this point. There I was, with my braces and the rubber bands lined up in my mouth again, and I realized something inconceivable: Boys are only human, too. They're not invincible superheroes or unapproachable monsters—they're just boys. And so I was never afraid to talk to a boy again. On the contrary, I slowly transformed from an ugly duckling into a beautiful swan. But I've never forgotten what it's like not to always be the center of attention and to feel more on the fringes of society. Trust me, that's not a nice feeling. I often think back on this story and have to laugh out loud, and I will always remember Nick as my braces-and-rubber-band hero.

When I (accidentally!) locked my biology teacher in

I was about twelve, and it was a Friday. Biology was on the schedule—and no, I wasn't exactly obsessed with cell nuclei and bone structures. But our biology teacher was nice. Not a cool, lab-coat-wearing rock star, but the quiet, friendly type, a bit older, but likable. The lessons were okay—not my favorite subject, but engaging enough that I didn't completely check out.

The biology room was set up like a small lecture hall: The tables rose in tiers, row after row, like a mini-theater for dissecting frogs, looking through microscopes, and there was Paul, the skeleton. In the back, a door led to a mysterious storage room. Inside, there were preserved animals in jars, biology textbooks, models, and all sorts of strange specimens. In short: the real core of biological science.

That day, at the end of the lesson, I was searching for my eraser, which meant I was the last one in the room. Everyone else had already left, including the teacher. At least, that's what I thought.

The door to the storage room was open, and I heard a voice from inside. "Goodbye!" I called out politely. "Please close the door!" came the reply. Of course, I thought. I'm a neat person. So, I closed the storage room door securely—and the classroom door behind me, as I was supposed to. Then I left.

On the way to the bus stop, a fleeting thought crossed my mind: Hmm... was that really the right door? But the teacher had told me to. So I was sure. Why would he sit in a room that couldn't be opened from the inside? That sounded absurd.

Well, it wasn't absurd. It was reality. The storage room had no windows. And—surprise—the door could only be opened from the outside.

So now my teacher was stuck in a windowless room, sharing the space with Paul the skeleton and a dozen pickled frogs in jars. Only the small couch made it even remotely comfortable. Of course, I knew it was Friday. I just didn't think twice about it and was convinced everything was fine. And so, he had to pass the time in illustrious company.

Fortunately, he was discovered before the weekend actually began. The janitor was doing his rounds and heard the knocking and shouting. So, my biology teacher didn't have to spend his Friday night among alcohol-preserved frogs and Paul.

On Monday morning, the class was asked who had closed the door. I immediately raised my hand because I didn't want anyone else to get in trouble. I simply said, "He told me to close the door."

The teachers realized it wasn't done with malicious intent—and it was then clearly stated that, from now on, only the teacher was allowed to close the storage room door. I think this story has made it into the school archives forever. And honestly? It could have been worse. Some people make history; I accidentally lock teachers in rooms. But at least I did it with style. And Paul.

After graduating, I went back to the university to earn a few more credits for my teaching internship. I was walking down the hallway, minding my own business, when a professor suddenly stepped out of an office, looked at me, and said, "Oh, Ms. Eckel!"

I stopped, surprised. So many students over so many years, and he recognized me right away? He smiled and simply said, "You're not easily forgotten." And that wasn't the first or last time I heard that sentence.

Why I went to a brothel during a student exchange

When you're in seventh grade and taking French, a student exchange program to France is practically mandatory. I was really looking forward to it—finally, my first trip abroad without my parents. This is going to be fun, I thought. Oh yes. It was. But... not the way I expected. As is customary in our family—especially among the women—my mother had another one of those... well... inspirations. She asked, “What will you do if no one picks you up?” I was taken aback. “If no one picks me up? Why wouldn’t anyone pick me up?” We had exchanged letters, our teacher was there, everything was organized! So why the strange question? But my mother said dryly, “I just have a gut feeling. As if no one will pick you up.”

To be honest, that gave me a little knot in my stomach, because I knew my mother. Her ‘gut feelings’ had a nasty track record. But I pushed it aside. I hopped on the bus, and off we went. The trip was great. We had tons of cassettes with us (yes, really), the bus driver was funny, and the atmosphere was just fantastic. When we finally arrived, we got off, retrieved our suitcases, and lined up in rows. In front of us: lots of families, lots of children, lots of hugs. One by one, they were picked up. I thought to myself, “Well, I don’t have to be first.” Then, “Okay, at least half are still here...” Then, “Wait... am I seriously the last one?”

And yes. I was. I stood there, alone with the two teachers. It was a truly embarrassing moment. My teacher looked at me, then at the empty space around me, and just said, “That’s strange. That’s never happened before.” And I just thought, “You’re not serious...” He looked at me and said with a grin, “But who’s involved again, of course? Ms. Eckel!” Back then, it was just Miss... ha ha ha. I just thought, “Ms. Eckel strikes again, of course, the biology door affair.” There was a flurry of phone calls. Back then, there were no cell phones, so it took a while. After what felt like three years, a family finally arrived. With them was a girl, two or three years older than me, and it showed. We drove to her house. I even got my own room, so everything was fine. Except that she had a slightly different list of priorities: boys, boys, boys.

I found boys interesting, too, but honestly, not to the extent that she did. Nevertheless, I came to terms with it. We went to parties, I went to school with her, everything was exciting. And then came the day of the legendary trip. We had a small, cool clique that we hung out with. And as is often the case, at some point nature calls, it was time for a bathroom break. I grabbed a buddy and we looked for a public restroom. None in sight. But there was a building with a sign that looked like a hotel. We went inside and politely asked in our best school French if we could just… well… "Toilette, s'il vous plaît?"

There was a woman sitting at the bar. And apart from that, there were only men. Well dressed. Sitting in armchairs. With that "I'm waiting for something" look on their faces. The woman grinned strangely, said something (much too fast for our French) and waved us toward the restroom. We just thought how nice the place was. A bit of a strange atmosphere, but nice. So we went to the bathroom and did what we had to do. My buddy came out and casually said, "By the way, I peed in the sink—it was kind of weird with the toilet signs." Great stuff. We laughed. Our friends were already waiting outside. Of course, they immediately asked, "Where were you guys?!" And we just said, "Oh, in there. It was weird."

And then it dawned on us:

Red lighting. A sign that did not say 'hotel.'

The men.

The woman.

The look.

The atmosphere.

This was not a hotel.

We had been in a brothel.

Yep. Two well-behaved German exchange students, naively looking for a toilet, ended up in a French brothel. And who was right in the middle of it all, of course? Ms. Eckel!

This story spread like wildfire. And it was still being told many years later. At class reunions. At family gatherings. At every occasion where someone mentioned the word "France" or "toilet." Today, I can laugh about it. Some people go on student exchanges and come back with souvenirs. I came back with a story for life. And—as always—with style. And a slight toilet trauma. And no—that wasn't my last trip to France.

I actually went there a second time. And again, I wasn't picked up. Why? My pen pal was pregnant. By the mailman. Yes. Of course. Ms. Eckel strikes again.

Lost in the British Museum

I was fifteen, and it was our class trip to London—and yes, I was stoked. Not because of the fish and chips or Buckingham Palace, but because the British Museum was on the itinerary. Just the thought of it made my history-loving heart race. Mummies! Romans! Things a thousand years old that were still intact! I was ready. Inside, it was huge. No, huge isn't the right word. Gigantic. Halls full of light, shadows, glass, statues, corridors, staircases, rooms with things as ancient as the sand in my geography book. I was glued to the display cases like a moth to a spotlight. Our group moved on—but I didn't. I stopped at an ancient Egyptian sarcophagus and thought: "Wow, it has better cheekbones than I do."

And then—silence. I looked up. No one there. The whole group was gone. My teacher? Vanished. Just me, a few tourists, and a rather smug-looking stone lion. I panicked. The museum is a labyrinth of civilizations. I started running—brave at first, then slightly desperate. Up the stairs. Down again. Up again. Everything looked the same somehow. Statues, halls, doors. At one point, I thought: Maybe they accidentally put me on display with the Romans? In my desperation, I bolted down a staircase. And suddenly there was no more grand hall. No shiny floor. No whispering school groups. Only silence. And dust. And shelves. And artifacts. Everywhere. Bags, wooden boxes, rolled-up carpets, drawers with labels, mysterious and dusty—a temporary storage facility or archive, whatever it was. And me in the middle of it all. Fifteen years old. Accidentally in the forbidden zone.

For the first time in my life, I was genuinely scared. Not just a little "Oh crap, how do I get out of here?" but a real, prickly unease. The kind of goosebumps you get when the door slams shut, the light flickers, and you're in the semi-darkness, surrounded by things that shouldn't actually feel alive. I didn't know if an alarm was about to go off or if a mummy was going to shout "Boo!" At some point, I thought: "If I don't find my way out of here soon, I'll turn to dust myself. And in 500 years, an intern will find me with the label 'Type: stray school visitor, condition: semi-serious.'" But another part of me found it absolutely fascinating. It was as if I had found the museum's matrix. The secret basement of history. Where things are kept that no one is (yet) supposed to see. I ventured a few steps forward—it creaked. Something was glittering in a glass box.

Despite all my nervousness, something was awakened in me right there, in that mix of shock, amazement, and dust, because the feeling I had back then has stayed with me to this day. I wanted to know where things came from, why they were preserved, how they were found. And that's exactly why I later studied archaeology. Fortunately, I eventually found a door. And a staircase. I ran up, heart pounding, crept past an ancient mosaic fragment reminiscent of the Byzantine exhibitions, and there—finally—I heard voices and saw my group.

Everyone was there. The teacher was just turning around, probably to alert the museum management. I trotted over inconspicuously, pretending everything was fine. "Where were you?" he asked. I said, "Uh... I took a quick dive into deep archaeology." He looked at me like I was a rare find. I blushed. And thought to myself: "Typical me. One moment of inattention and I'm already lost in 10,000 years of human history."

The Red Flash—A Fiesta with a life of its own

I drove up to Betzenberg on a normal afternoon—not a game day, just after practice. My goal was simple: get a few jerseys and balls signed. I had collected them from other fans who, of course, knew I was acquainted with all the players. After all, I was Horst Eckel's daughter. And word gets around. I parked my Ford Fiesta—my famous "Red Flash"—and headed for the players' parking lot, right where the pros always exit after training. A few fans were already waiting, but I positioned myself right in the front. Balls and jerseys in hand, a huge smile on my face—and yes, to be honest, I felt pretty great because I knew the guys would greet me when they came out. And they certainly did. One after the other emerged, called my name, laughed, and signed autographs. This was my moment. I was on cloud nine. I was surrounded mainly by female fans, and I could feel their envious stares. Rightly so—I belonged there. I was truly in the mix, not just standing by. And as is typical for me, whenever I reach such a peak of euphoria, it usually isn't long before I come crashing back down to earth. And with a huge thud.

Full of enthusiasm, I got into my "Red Flash." I rolled down the windows, cranked up the music, put my hand on the steering wheel, and tried to drive off with a flourish—the queen of the scene. All that was missing was a royal wave. But instead of first gear, I slammed it into reverse. And kissed the post behind me. Right there at Betzenberg. Not a flimsy metal post, but a beautiful, solid stone column, one of those supporting the stadium. Now it also bore the imprint of my car's rear end. The bang was impossible to ignore. And the laughter? Definitely on the side of the soccer players and the female fans.

I had nothing to laugh about, as I was probably as red as a beet and just thought: "Dear God, let me sink into the ground." I would have loved to put the car in first gear and speed away as fast as possible. Unfortunately, that wasn't an option. I was stuck to the post. So, I had no choice but to get out of the car and fully expose myself to the embarrassment.

Thank goodness cell phones weren't around back then to go viral. I surely would have been the laughingstock of the century. It was surreal enough as it was.

The trunk was crushed and jammed open. It wouldn't close. The players, who had just been signing autographs, now fetched ropes. Yes, ropes. One guy looked for an old banner rope, the next improvised a kind of knot-solution that looked more like performance art. One person held the trunk lid shut, another pulled the rope through my Fiesta, and outside, someone else stood and tied a double knot as if mooring a fishing boat. I stood beside them, no longer feeling like a queen, but like a fish out of water. With a bright red face. I tried to salvage what little dignity I could so I could flee the scene of my defeat as quickly as possible.

So I got into my dented Fiesta, made myself as small as possible, and drove off. As I collapsed inwardly just like my trunk lid, all I could think was: Oh man, how am I going to explain this to my father? And even today—yes, truly—if you look closely at Betzenberg, you'll find a red stripe on one of the posts. It was left there by the "Red Flash." And by one of the most embarrassing but also funniest moments of my life.

Shopping cart of horror

It wasn't quite as public as my pole crash at Betzenberg, but it was embarrassing enough to earn a spot in my personal collection of awkward moments. I was just doing some harmless shopping. Completely ordinary, completely unspectacular. At least, that's what I thought. I had a shopping cart, pushed it through the aisles, and tossed in a few items—butter, fruit, something with oats—the usual sensible food. But as is often the case in such moments, my mind was miles away. I was daydreaming—as I always do—about Munich. I imagined scenes, played out entire dialogues in my head, walking through streets, talking to people, maybe sitting in a café and working on something important. In short, I was far removed from the reality of a supermarket in the here and now. My body was pushing the cart, and my mind was strolling through Schwabing.

At some point—apparently during a particularly intense phase of this daydream—I abandoned my shopping cart and grabbed a new one. I was convinced it was mine. After all, it was standing exactly where I expected it to be. So I pushed off, without a doubt, as a matter of course. I noticed people were looking at me a little strangely. Not outright staring, but looking a little irritated. The kind of look that makes you think, "What's wrong with me or with them?" I decided on the latter, of course. It wasn't until I was unloading my groceries at the checkout that I noticed. I looked into the cart and my breath caught in my throat. It wasn't just full. It was packed to the brim. With liquor. Only liquor. Bottle after bottle. Vodka, liqueur, rum, herbal bitters—a whole assortment of spirits, like the inventory for a club party.

I stood there, my face bright red, stammering, "Uh... that's not mine. Really! I... mine is... it's back there!" The cashier looked at me as if to say, "Yeah, yeah, that's what they all say." Behind me, people were already starting to whisper. I saw an elderly gentleman frown and a woman shake her head, ever so slightly. I raced off, pushed the liquor cart back at top speed—almost grazing half the candy section in the process—and arrived just in time to prevent a store employee from starting to put the contents of the cart back on the shelves. "I... accidentally... uh... took this... it's not mine." She nodded politely, but with one of those looks that tells you she'll be telling this story at dinner tonight.

So I fetched my shopping cart—the one with the wholesome oat stuff—and got back in line at the checkout. In the same line, of course. With the same looks, of course. People were now looking at me the way you look at someone who is trying to wriggle out of a blatant lie. I could literally hear what they were thinking: "Aha, switched from alcohol to oats—very credible." What can I say? It was exactly one of those moments when you sink deep into your thoughts, and when you finally surface, you want to disappear into the ground immediately.

When I accidentally ended up in the warm-up pool

It was 1997, and the air at the stadium was electric. 1. FC Kaiserslautern had just clinched a promotion to the Bundesliga, filling the stands with red-and-white euphoria. As usual, I was on the sidelines, just a regular spectator in my black-and-white jumpsuit, with no official role.

Then, a player, utterly drenched in sweat and beaming with joy, locked eyes with me. I immediately sensed trouble. Before I could object, he had me tucked under his arm—like a piece of salami, if you can believe it. I struggled, clawing desperately at the edges of the catacombs, my fingernails sacrificing themselves in vain resistance. But it was no use. Moments later, with a SPLASH, I was submerged in the warm-up pool.

Fully clothed—jumpsuit, shoes, everything—I landed among the players, tossed in like a forgotten gym towel. When I finally came up for air, I noticed the black streaks from my shoe soles clinging to the edge of the pool. I hadn't just made an impression; I'd left a tangible mark.

I was quickly handed an improvised outfit: oversized pants that nearly reached my chest and ill-fitting flip-flops, accompanied by a few pitying glances. Shivering, dripping wet, and having shed all dignity, I shuffled toward the VIP room. The elevator ride was a journey of shame and dampness, punctuated by the slap-slap of the flip-flops.

The elevator doors opened, and everyone turned. There I stood: the unintentional celebrity of the day. My father, who was already there, couldn't help but grin. Who else could boast of entering the VIP box after a game with the sophisticated style of a drowned cat?

The truth is, I wasn't part of the team, and I didn't get a medal. But I was the only person who had literally left their mark on the warm-up pool tiles that day. And today, when someone mentions the enduring black streak on the pool's edge, I can proudly claim it. My father's likely reaction? A smile, and a proud, "That's my daughter for you."

When a Man Crashes Through the Ceiling

It was a typical Sunday in 2006, the day felt like Grandma's warm chocolate pudding—soft, sweet, cozy. I was stretched out on my bed, surrounded by pillows, remote control in hand, half snuggled up, half awake, completely absorbed in a movie. I was watching The Glass Bottom Boat, featuring Doris Day. As always, she was romantic, funny, and full of charm, with that light, bouncy, tongue-in-cheek sparkle that only she had. She stumbled charmingly, getting stuck with a workman in an umbrella stand, both of them tangled up, half frightened, half indignant, but of course with dignity. It was a classic Doris Day moment as she stumbled from one faux pas to the next, but always with style, always with an enchanting smile that transformed every embarrassment into something brilliant.

I smiled. Could happen to me, too, I thought, slightly amused.

Oh yes, it could... Suddenly, I heard a scratching noise above me. I looked up. Rooftop sparrows? A cat? Perhaps a particularly curious marten? Then the scratching turned into a rumble. And the rumble to a real, unmistakable, no longer to be ignored ominous crack. My head and my gaze wandered up very slowly.

CRRRRRRAAACK!

I could hardly believe my eyes, because a man fell through the middle of my ceiling and landed directly in front of my bed. Yes, really. Dusty, frightened, completely out of nowhere. Not on the bed, but very close to it, so close that my bedspread fluttered for a moment as if in slow motion. I sat there perfectly straight. Doris Day was just falling into a goldfish tank while I looked back and forth between the TV, the remote control, and the man on the floor. My brain desperately tried to make sense of the scene.

The man sat up slowly. Blinked. Got up, dusted himself off. Then he said: “Oh... sorry.” I didn't say anything. What do you say when a stranger suddenly falls through the ceiling? Then he stammered: “I forgot my keys.” Oh, I see, I thought. Well then. No problem. That would have been my first thought, too, to dive headfirst through the ceiling instead of ringing the doorbell.

What I did say was: “Oh... but this is my apartment.” He looked around, puzzled, and seemed more concerned with trying to get his bearings. It's not easy to digest the fact that you've just fallen through a ceiling into a complete stranger's bedroom. He looked to the right, then to the left, blinked slightly dazed at the ceiling, from which bits of plaster were still gently falling, and seemed to be asking himself: Nice dream, am I awake yet? Is ther any coffee?

Then he raised his eyes, put on a smile as if this were the most normal thing in the world, and said: “Would you like to go for a coffee?” Perhaps some people would have responded with a flirtatious glance. I, however, was close to offering him my pillow as a return ticket. I swear, my facial expression was somewhere between shock and total inner confusion. Coffee? Now?

It turned out that he was my new neighbor who had recently moved in. Three apartments, right next to each other. His to the left, mine in the middle, and our landlord's to the right. Who, by the way, was even home that Sunday. So he could have just rung the bell, as a first resort. But no. The young American decided to climb through a small hatch into the suspended ceiling that connected across all three apartments, foolishly believing that this would allow him to reach his apartment. But that was impossible, because there was no access from there. Why he got so lost in this dimly lit cavity on a mere 10 square feet that he ended up crashing through my ceiling remains a mystery to me today.

I then spent a whole week with a makeshift tarp over my bed. Fine plaster would trickle down with every little gust of wind, and I didn't need the air conditioning, especially since it was not even summer, but winter. Oh, and I actually did end up going for coffee with him, because my brain was still running on a kind of post-traumatic autopilot and I just stumbled along. After my third sip of cappuccino, I slowly came to my senses and calmly explained to him, after he asked me out on another date, that I was not keen on sequels or further such scenes and that I would like to continue my life without holes in the ceiling and dates with airborne neighbors.

In short, I was friendly, but very clear. And he got it. I think even Doris Day would have nodded slightly at this point, charmingly pushed the bill toward him, and then floated out of the scene with an enchanting, ladylike smile. Unfortunately, I was not granted such a cinematic departure. I would have liked to walk away like Doris Day, with my head held high, a jaunty sway of my hips, and a charming roll of my eyes. Instead, I stumbled back out of the scene more or less gracefully, slightly distraught, but trying to keep my composure.

The young man had long since disappeared, probably somewhere at a safe distance from any form of ceiling architecture. I, on the other hand, was still sitting there, a bit stunned. Then I finally got up and left the café without further interruption. At least that was my intention.

But at the door, a resolute waitress caught up with me and asked with a raised eyebrow whether I just wanted to drink the cappuccino or pay for it as well. Apparently, my involuntary companion had also forgotten his wallet in his fright, or thought that the fall through the ceiling was invitation enough. So he left behind a complete package, unfortunately, without the right of return. A hole for free, hassle included. The bill? Ignored. And the dirt? I had to work for hours to clear it all up. It was so excessive that I briefly considered charging admission: "Welcome to the Museum of Modern Disasters." I paid, apologized, smiled awkwardly, and wondered why it was always me who ended up in situations like this. Since then, I have considered ceilings more treacherous than doors, because doors can at least be locked. When it comes to ceilings, apparently, the only thing that helps is prayer or a helmet.

My big moment on the red carpet

It was during the 2006 World Cup, at a game between Saudi Arabia and Spain in Kaiserslautern's Betzenberg stadium. King Juan Carlos of Spain was also there, and we had seats very close to him. The second half was a long way off, so my father and I headed toward the VIP area during the break. My father went ahead while I quickly ran back to my seat to grab my bag. That day, I was wearing a very elegant but, unfortunately, extremely dangerous pair of pants—wide, soft, and flowing, a real fashion statement. Unfortunately, they were also a safety hazard.

The stairs were covered with a lavish red carpet—classy, regal, and slippery. I knew reporters were waiting below. I also knew my father was already waiting. So I tried to combine both: elegance with efficiency. The art of being fast yet stylish. In my head, the whole thing was already playing out like a movie scene. I envisioned myself, almost floating down the steps with graceful, light strides, upright posture, chin slightly raised, and a calm gaze. I felt fantastic at that moment, a mix of a Hollywood diva and a visiting head of state. I had a clear picture in my mind: downstairs with the reporters, I would nod discreetly and regally. A hint of acknowledgment, as if I were responding to their respectful gaze with a silent, "Thank you, yes, I know." Then I would glide elegantly toward the VIP area, my movements fluid and dignified—a brief appearance, but one that would leave an impression.

But as so often happens when I start looking forward to a moment like this—when I internally pat myself on the back before anything has even occurred—it happens: my personal, almost traditional mishap. My foot got caught in my own pant leg. Before I even understood what was happening, I transformed from a high-society lady into a human snowball. I fell—no, I slid—down the stairs in a kind of acrobatic pirouette, a mix between a ballerina and a bowling ball. When I reached the bottom, I was sitting on my backside. On the red carpet. Right in front of a group of reporters who, like me, were motionless. A collective freeze, probably out of surprise, perhaps also from politely suppressed vicarious embarrassment.

Then, out of nowhere, an old-school gentleman stepped forward: Franz Beckenbauer. Yes, Franz Beckenbauer! He just happened to be standing right at the bottom of the stairs, perhaps as part of fate's plan, to save me from total embarrassment. With the utmost composure and a charming smile, he held out his hand to me and said, "Oops! Who do we have here?" Of course, he knew me and knew who I was. But it was also perfectly clear: he would have helped anyone else in the same way. With a quick, elegant pull, he helped me to my feet as if nothing had happened. No smirks, no comments, just an act of chivalry.

Then he took me to my father, who, thank goodness, hadn't noticed the fall, or at least pretended not to. Franz took the ridiculousness out of the whole moment, and I was deeply grateful to him for that. I think even the reporters collectively decided not to exploit the moment. Perhaps out of respect for 'Der Kaiser'. Perhaps also out of shock. I still enjoy telling this story today—with a wink and a lot of gratitude, because Franz Beckenbauer was not only a soccer legend but also a true gentleman. And a loyal friend of my father's. Embarrassing? No. More like one of those moments when you speak and the whole room falls silent. I don't even know if this moment should be classified as embarrassing, per se. Perhaps more as a moment that started out silently, that then quickly crescendoed into a spectacle, albeit with dignity. And with applause in one's own head.

Standing up against disrespect

It was one of those long, dignified, somewhat tedious evenings: the Steiger Award presentation. My father was to be honored. He, the hero of 1954, the world champion maker, now over 80 years old, was being recognized for his life's work. And rightly so. The honor came late in the evening, but it came. The laudatory speech was given; everything was very official. The audience was a mix of celebrities, prominent figures, politicians, and the press. My father came onto the stage as the evening's main event—literally the "crowning glory"—tired but standing tall. It was his moment.

But as he made his way to the stage, something happened that still makes my hair stand on end today: at the next table—occupied by prominent figures, politicians, decision-makers, the kind of people who love to be seen but rarely actually listen—there was talking. Not whispering. Not respectful nodding. No: talking. Commenting. Laughing. While my father walked across the stage, while the laudatory speech was winding down, they just kept talking. I sat there, heard it, everyone heard it, and thought, "Seriously?"

It wasn't just loud. It was aggressively loud. Disrespectfully loud. In that moment, it was perfectly clear to me: I had to go over there. Not because I love being the center of attention, but because otherwise, I would've exploded. So I stood up—with the composure of someone who has nothing left to lose—walked over to the table of the tone-deaf, leaned forward, and said in a voice that invited no discussion, only delivered impact: "I just wanted to say that I honestly find it quite disrespectful when my father—who is over 80 years old, after all he has done for this country—comes on stage here to be honored for his life's work, and this table thinks it's okay to talk loudly. It's simply inappropriate."

Silence. Complete, piercing, uncomfortably ringing silence.

I turned around with the self-assured stance of a daughter who knew exactly why she had just stood up. I sat back down in my seat. Back straight. Chin up. No hesitation. No regret. No remorse. Anyone who hurts the people I love had better start praying.

Four butts, a bush, and me

It was a freezing cold winter evening on the Betzenberg. The sky was an inky blue, breath hung in the air like fog, and the stadium floodlights cut through the early evening like stage spotlights. I was excited. It was a special game, and I had been looking forward to it all day. I had parked my car right out front, directly on the street, with only a narrow strip of grass and dense bushes separating me from the view of the stadium. I was still sitting in the car, letting the heater hum quietly, reapplying my lipstick, and checking my reflection in the rearview mirror. The VIP entrance wasn't far—just across the street, a few steps through the crowd. I was just about to get out when they suddenly appeared. Four guys. Out of nowhere. I hadn't seen them coming. They walked up the street from below, turned into the parking lot, and headed purposefully for the small strip of grass—right between my car and the bushes.

Before I even really understood what was happening, all four of them dropped their pants and started urinating. Right in front of my windshield. In the floodlights. And when I say "right in front," I mean their legs were against my bumper. If I had stretched my arm through the window, I could have pinched their butts. They were that close. I sat there, frozen. Four bare butts in the stadium floodlights. Less than six feet from my face. I wasn't just shocked; I was perplexed. The scene was so absurd that I almost had to laugh in a mixture of anger, disbelief, and bewilderment. They hadn't even glanced around. They hadn't checked to see if anyone was sitting in the car. If anyone was walking by. And a lot of people were: women, children, families—all on their way to the stadium.

Some saw the scene directly, others only out of the corner of their eyes, but everyone sensed that something was completely wrong here. A woman quickly pulled her child close to her. An elderly gentleman paused briefly, then shook his head and walked on. Two teenage girls quietly giggled as they clearly recorded the scene to show their friends. A man grinned furtively when he met my gaze, then ducked away. I sat there like Doris Day in an absurd Hollywood movie. Except that Cary Grant was missing. And instead, there were four backsides standing in the floodlights. And like Doris Day, I acted: quickly, charmingly, and absolutely cinematic.

I reached for the horn. Not hesitantly. Not half-heartedly.

BEEP!

The effect was priceless. All four jumped into the air at the same time. One jerked so hard that he almost pulled his pants over his head. Another stumbled halfway into the bushes. Belt buckles clattered, beer bottles swayed, and a collective chaos of hurriedness and embarrassment unfolded right in front of my hood. Then they finally saw me. In the car. Frowning. Lipstick perfect. And with a look that said, "I saw everything. And yes—it was me." Three of them disappeared as quickly as they had appeared. The fourth, however, remained and simply continued urinating. Slowly. Persistently. He didn't even turn around. Just a weary glance over his shoulder that said, "It doesn't matter now."

I got out with my shoulders straight and my bag under my arm. I walked briskly toward the street, heading for the stadium, and felt the stares of at least ten people who had just stored the scene in their memory. Two women nodded at me with a grin. A man secretly clapped his hands. I heard someone quietly whisper to his buddy, "The one with the horn, right?" Yes. That was me, because sometimes a horn is not just a horn, but an act of self-respect. A signal to the world: "Not with me, guys. And definitely not in front of my car." And those four butts? They totally deserved it.

As you can see, a lot has happened to me over the years—embarrassing moments, minor dramas, situations that make you laugh, shake your head, and want to tell others about them. But then there are those other moments. The ones you don't laugh about. The ones that quietly haunt you, even years later. Not because they were loud or spectacular, but because they show you where you could have been the bigger person, more human, more compassionate.

The first moment that comes to mind was when I was seven years old and in second grade. A girl from the village came up to me and asked for my help. I liked her, but she lived on a farm, and I don't know how to express this without being rude or hurtful, and I don't want to be either of those things. But as a child, you have other things on your mind. I just thought: No, I don't want to help and get so close to her. You can smell the cows. I helped her, but not as I should have. When she left, she pressed herself against the wallpaper on the stairs, and then you could see these dark marks from her hand. I didn't say anything to her, I didn't insult her, but I just couldn't help her the way I should have. But this person, this girl, was strong, and she went her own way. I take my hat off to her for never giving up despite all the hurdles.

The second moment was when I was fifteen. I was always a little possessive of my mother because I loved her very much. A girl who lived at the end of Vogelbach and whose mother was seriously ill always ran the whole way to the train station. It was very far, especially in the morning when it was still dark. My mother took her with her. So she came to our house, and when my mom drove me to the train station in the morning, she took her along. Actually, that was a given for my mother, and it should have been a given for me too. But somehow I was jealous. I can't explain why. I had no reason. I didn't show it, at least not to the girl, but I think she sensed it because she was in a situation where you have to be very sensitive. She didn't come anymore.

A friend of mine also said, "Dagmar, you're reacting completely wrong." She was right. Of course I reacted wrong, and I was truly sorry, and I am still truly sorry, even now, after so many years. I hope that she found her way despite all the obstacles. I would like to apologize to her officially here. Maybe she'll read it someday. But I also learned from it. Today, I would react differently.

Horst as a schoolboy

Horst as a child, aged 8

Dad skiing

Wedding photo of Host and Hannelore

Horst asks Hanne to dance
at the fair in 1952

Die Braut des Weltmeisters

Das Mädchen Hannelore ist nun eine glückliche Frau. Aber auch eine mutige: Oder gehört etwa kein Mut dazu, einen deutschen Nationalspieler zu heiraten? In den letzten Jahren jedenfalls mußten die Fußballbräute unserer Nationalelf mehr Niederlagen miterleiden, als Siege mitfeiern ... Trotzdem wagte es Hannelore Schey (20) und schritt in Kaiserslautern mit Weltmeisterschaftsspieler Horst Eckel vor den Altar. Fritz Walter war Trauzeuge — und überbrachte auch die Glückwünsche von Sepp Herberger. Unser Glückwunsch dem jungen Paar. Ehemänner sind bessere Fußballer ... — von der F jedenfalls waren fast alle verheiratet.

Erster Schritt ins Eheleben: Horst Eckel und seine Hannelore

Newspaper article Wedding

Aunt Ilse with cousin Irene and uncle Robert

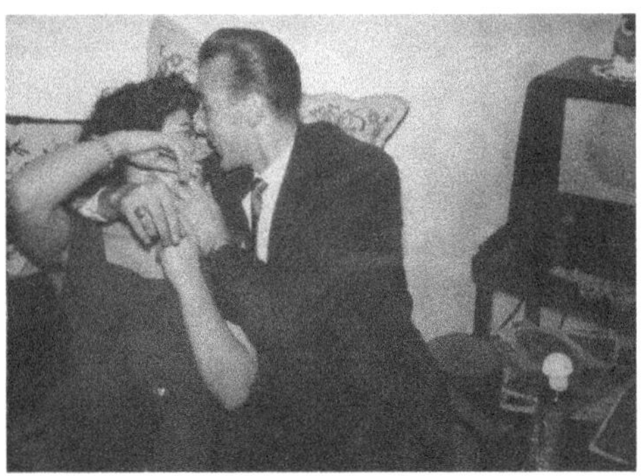

My parents as a young married couple

Horst and his father Richard

Horst with father-in-law Mathias

Horst dancing at home with
my cousin Irene Twist

Host with his first car

Dad picking apples

My mother at Lake Constance

Host in his bathrobe
at Lake Constance

Hannelore with her sister Ilse
and Uncle Robert

Horst in swimming trunks

Horst and Hanne playing
on vacation Miniature golf

Dagmar as a baby

Dad teaches me to ride a bike
1973

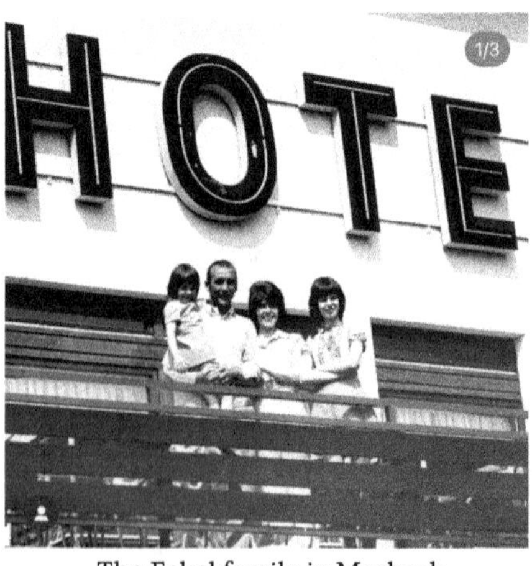

The Eckel family in Morbach

Dagmar with her school cone

Dagmar Spring 1980

Letter from America 1980

Letter from America 1980

Walt Disney tickets 1980

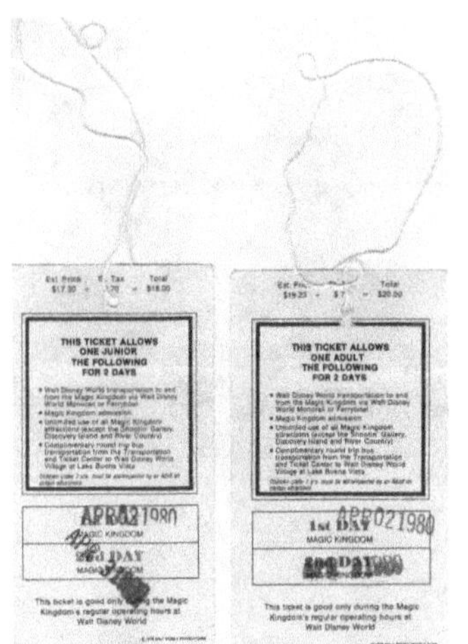

Walt Disney tickets

Dagmar Autumn 1981

Dagmar 1983

Winter vacation in Saas Fee 1983

Dagmar 1986

Dagmar in the fireplace room 1989

Summer vacation in Cannes, 1986

Dagmar, 1990

Dagmar, 1991

Dagmar, summer 1991

Dagmar, 1994

Horst, Hanne, and Dagmar
befor the cup match, 1997

Carnival celebration

Hannelore at the bazaar in Tunisia

1986

Horst Hanne Dagmar

Grandmother Emilie on her mother's side

Horst Tennis

Horst and Hannelore

Dad always in action

Horst and Hannelore

Dad loved barbecuing

Playing foosball with Dad in 2019

Total Vacation—Full Speed Ahead Into Chaos

America! For many, it's a land of unlimited opportunities. For us, however, it's the country where we quickly realized that even those unlimited opportunities couldn't change the fact that the Eckel family couldn't escape chaos, even on another continent. I was eleven years old when we first flew to Miami to visit friends. The anticipation was huge: America! Palm trees! Cheeseburgers! The Statue of Liberty! Roller coasters! So, jet-lagged and eager for adventure, we landed in good spirits at our friends' place in Florida. It was quickly decided that we would, of course, visit the famous Walt Disney World in Orlando. What was a childhood dream come true for others became... well, a turning point for us.

The Mount Everest of nervous breakdowns

Our mission was clear: Space Mountain. The legendary indoor roller coaster in total darkness. Just stars, speed, and a complete loss of control. My mom, my sister, and I were determined to psych ourselves up. My dad, ever the pragmatist, warned us: "I don't think this is for you." But of course, we weren't going to let that stop us. "Tsss, dad. We're brave. We can handle it." What we underestimated was the three-hour wait. Three hours in an endless, snaking line of sweaty families, hyperventilating teenagers, and people wearing glowing Mickey Mouse ears who were already laughing hysterically. The closer we got to the entrance, the more our excitement gave way to sheer panic. There was this strange, deep rumbling sound echoing through the hall. The people coming back from the ride didn't look like heroes. They looked like survivors. I looked at my sister. She was white as a sheet. My mother grabbed my hand. I just wanted to get out. But it was too late. There were already new crowds of people behind us. There was no turning back. So we stayed and waited another hour in the semi-darkness, surrounded by flashing displays and beeping machines.

When it was finally our turn, my mother said, "We're not going." Just like that. I said, "Yeah, me neither." And my sister just nodded silently. The employee looked at us as if we were a bizarre special case. But she smiled professionally and escorted us out through a side exit, past the "real" passengers who looked at us with a mix of pity and mockery. Our father was waiting outside, grinning broadly and he said, "Didn't I tell you?" Three hours of waiting, and we hadn't rode an inch. But we were wiser for the experience, and our pride was still standing in the line.

The day five teenagers climbed over my bed

There are some evenings in life you never want to forget. And then there are the ones you'll never forget because they're so utterly absurd that even the script of a Doris Day comedy seems like a tax form by comparison. This evening was the latter. We were on vacation with friends, somewhere between sunshine, the pool, and the vague hope of spending three days without drama. Our hosts were nice and had two sons our age. One of them, let's call him Thomas, was a classic: way too cool for school, hair like a shampoo commercial, and always on the hunt for an opportunity to party. That evening, he got one: the house to himself. All the adults were gone, and for Thomas, that was practically a national holiday.

While music was already pumping through the walls in the rest of the house, my sister and I were lying in our room. The reason? My sister had gotten a sunburn that ranged somewhere between freshly cooked lobster and fire engine red. Neither of us was in the mood to party. No makeup, no dancing, no desire. “We'll just stay here,” I said. “We can hear the music anyway.” “And we'll probably smell the alcohol soon, too,” my sister muttered. We thought we'd have peace and quiet. We thought we were smart. But we hadn't factored in the window. It was around 9:30 p.m. We were lying there, half-dozing, half-annoyed, when I suddenly saw something out of the corner of my eye. Something unusual. Something… foot-like. A foot. A real, male, rather confident foot pushed itself over the windowsill.

“Um… do you see that too?” I whispered to my sister. But before she could answer, it was too late: an entire guy climbed through the window. Not shy or embarrassed. No. He climbed over my bed as if it were the sidewalk he grew up on and calmly left the room through our door. I was speechless. So was my sister. We stared at each other, feeling perplexed and misplaced. Then came the next foot. And the next leg. Another one. He gave us a friendly nod, as if to say, “Don't worry, I'll be gone in a second.” And again: over my bed. Through the door and gone. Number three, four, and five—and slowly it was starting to feel personal. A total of five teenagers came through that window. Five!

Each of them with the nonchalant air of a resident. Some muttered a half-hearted hello, others smiled, one even offered me a bag of chips. I almost asked if I should be stamping their wrists, like at a club entrance. After the third one, it wasn't surreal anymore. It was just silly. We weren't even asked. We were just the thoroughfare. The scene was cinematic. It reminded me of a scene from the movie The Thrill of It All with Doris Day. It reminded me of those old movies where the heroine stands confused but charming in the midst of chaos. Except I didn't have a script, and there was no happy ending with a handsome Frenchman. I only had my bed, a window, and a parade of pubescent climbers who apparently didn't know what door handles were.

“Should we just close the window?” my sister asked at some point. I shrugged. “Then they'll probably break it.” In the end, it was kind of nice.

Somehow. Eventually, around midnight, it got quieter. No more feet. No more legs. No more chip bags. My sister fell asleep. I lay awake for a while. And I laughed. Quietly, but genuinely, because at some point, when you've had enough sunburns, lost wallets, and window parties, you realize: it's not the chaos that's annoying, it's the chaos that stays with you. This scene—five teenagers on a world tour over my bed—became one of my favorite vacation memories. And every time I see the movie The Pajama Game and Doris Day keeps her cool in her confused, charming way, I think: I was her. For just one evening.

Saas-Fee village: When the bunny hill becomes a dare

It began—like so many things in our family—with a plan we had shelved ages ago. The ski trip was planned years before, but as life would have it, my mother's slipped disc intervened. An operation, months of physical therapy, and the usual doctor's warnings about winter sports. So, project 'ski vacation' was postponed. And postponed. And, naturally, postponed again. Until 1983. I was fifteen by then, my mother's back was at least moderately stable, and the Eckel family decided to finally put their long-cherished plan into action. Destination: Saas-Fee, Switzerland. It sounds like a postcard scenery, with snow-covered roofs, glittering slopes, crunching snow, and mulled wine with whipped cream. Spoiler alert: It was nothing like that.

Up until then, the only 'boards' I'd stood on were in Morbach—and those were sliding devices, pure nostalgia. The hills there were gentle, easy, and totally kid-friendly. Saas-Fee, on the other hand, was… let's just say it was a whole new ball game. On the first day, my parents properly signed me up for ski lessons. With my heart hammering and my fingers numb, I stood on the so-called bunny hill, which looked more like an Olympic training venue to me. I somehow managed to stand up on the skis, which felt like two oversized, belligerent banana peels, and I tried to stay as upright as possible. Balance, technique, core strength—all words that meant absolutely nothing to me at that time.

The ski instructor watched me, frowned briefly, and then nodded as if he'd recognized something in me that I was completely unaware of. "She can go to the second class. Beginner level two." I—naive, optimistic, and silently praying—nodded and went along with it until I realized what "beginner level two" meant in Switzerland. My new group members were all only a few years older than me, but they had at least three winters of skiing under their belts. Some had already competed. They shot down the slopes like speed-demon ski bunnies, carving elegant slalom turns and executing textbook maneuvers. I just tried not to wipe out. I was basically always dead last.

The group regularly had to wait for me, which was about as enjoyable as a dental visit while doing a wall-sit. And the runs? A wall on the left, a cliff on the right, and in between, me with shaky knees and a panicked inner voice saying, "If you fall now, you'll roll all the way to Zurich." And all this knowing my father would eventually ask, "So? Did you have fun?" By the third day, I'd had enough. I couldn't do it anymore. Not physically, and certainly not mentally. That evening, I confessed to my parents. I was tired, drained, and angry at myself. I expected the classic Eckel reaction: just grit your teeth, don't give up, discipline, ambition, blah blah blah.

Instead, my father simply looked at me calmly, nodded, and said, "Then go to the ski instructor tomorrow and cancel. I'll come with you." What? Was that... understanding? Compassion? No lecture? The next day, we went to the ski instructor together. He listened to my story, looked at me like a teacher who suddenly finds an astrophysicist in his remedial math class, and said, "You've never had skis on before? Ever?" I shook my head. "Then you're a natural." My father grinned. "She's very athletic." I grinned too. And for the first time on this vacation, I felt like I had done something right, even though I had quit something.

Later, in the car, my father said something that has stayed with me to this day. Not condescending. Not lecturing. Just human. "Dagmar, your life is more important than any ski slope. There are limits, and those who recognize them often have more courage than those who blindly push past them." And there he was again: the father who always seemed strong but never wanted it at the expense of others, who taught me that you stay whole even when you back out, that courage doesn't always mean taking the steepest run, but sometimes just means saying out loud, "I can't do this anymore."

How my father accidentally became a ski instructor

After I decided to quit ski lessons—understandable after my involuntary extreme experience on the 'beginner's hill of death'—I looked for a new teacher: my father. He wasn't an official ski instructor, but in our family, the attribute "survived it" was often qualification enough. He also owned a neon-red ski suit so bright you could spot him from two miles away, even in the thickest snowstorm. To be honest, he looked exactly like a ski instructor: confident, leading the charge, calm in the chaos—a sort of Swiss Moses of the slopes with the charm of an Eckel and the courage of an experienced family man.

One of those days, we rode the gondola up the mountain together. At first, it was quiet, almost idyllic. The gondola swayed gently, the mountains beneath us looked like they were dusted with sugar, and I thought to myself that this was one of those moments people later romanticize as "the magic of winter" in family albums. Then the wind hit. And with it, the snow. Not just a light dusting. No, it was apocalypse mode: thick flakes sweeping horizontally across the view, gusts that made the gondola dance as if it were made of paper. We exchanged a look. Not a word was spoken, but we knew: this was not going to be a cozy afternoon of skiing.

When we reached the top, visibility was zero. We couldn't even see the tips of our own skis. The world was white, silent, and roaring all at once. And my father—the rock in the winter surf—just said, "Come on. We'll ski down slowly. Stay right behind me." The Red Lightning with his entourage. Easier said than done. He skied ahead like a silent leader into the white nothingness. I followed. And it worked. His red suit was my salvation, my point of reference, my lighthouse in a snowstorm.

What I didn't realize, however, was that I wasn't the only one who felt that way. More and more people lined up behind me. First two, then four, then seven—at some point we were a whole convoy, an avalanche of skiers clinging to my father's red suit like drowning people to a buoy. He didn't even notice until we reached the bottom, left the slope, and stood at the meeting point. The others practically threw their arms around him—"Merci, merci!"—and one even shouted: "You were the only one we could follow! Thank God you know your way around here, right?!" My father blinked, adjusted his zipper, and said dryly, "I'm a teacher—but actually, I teach German." And then that smile appeared. We all laughed. Not the polite smile of tourists in ski boots that are too tight. No, the real, deep-in-your-stomach laughter that comes when the snow finally stops whipping down, the sun tentatively fights its way through the clouds, and you realize you achieved something together.

And there it was again, the Eckel principle: you never truly plan for chaos, but when it happens, you make the best of it. If necessary, you simply turn your own father into a ski instructor for a stranded group of strangers who find comfort in his unshakeable calm and follow him blindly because, well, someone who looks like that must know what he's doing.

The result? I went on vacation to learn how to ski. Instead, I was almost swept off the slopes, internally skirted panic, and somehow made it to the bottom. No course in the world could have taught me that. But my father—in his red suit—showed me what real leadership is: don't shout, don't show off, just do the job. And if you have to, do it with half the ski resort in tow.

The domino effect and the frozen torn ligament

There are moments in life when you just want to prove yourself. To show you belong. To demonstrate that even after spinal disc surgery, you can easily keep up with all the fit skiers out there. For my mother, that moment arrived in the winter of 1983 in Saas-Fee on skis. A situation that, on its own, practically screams "over the top." "I can do that, too!" We were having one of those perfect, sunny ski days. The sky was an aggressively cheerful postcard blue, the snow a glistening shade that could only be described as "toothpaste white." My mother, who had been skiing quite cautiously until then, suddenly decided to make a statement. A declaration. An "I'm here, and I've got this!"

She stood at the top of a hill that probably felt like a small bump to her, but was actually quite steep. Her posture was determined, her balance courageously wobbly. Then, she set off. What followed was a mix of unexpected grace and pure terror. Her skis picked up speed. More speed than she wanted. She tried to brake—no luck. She wanted to turn, but it was too late. What she did next was pure instinct: she skied straight ahead, full speed, directly toward the lift station where a cozy crowd of people had gathered. It was like watching a slow-motion film. You could see her approaching, you could hear scattered cries of "Look out!", but no one had a chance. Then came the collision.

Bam!

One after another, they went down. Like dominoes. There was screaming, cursing, groaning, laughing—and right in the middle of it all was my mother, on her knees, her face bright red, apologizing, her words half-swallowed by the next wave of falling people. A single, chaotic pile of jackets, helmets, skis, and helpless bodies tangled together. It took several minutes for the mess of people and equipment to slowly untangle itself. Fortunately, no one seemed seriously injured, at least not at first.

At first, we were stunned, then completely overcome by laughter. It was like a slapstick comedy routine on skis: my mother limping but smiling. But while everyone else got back up, dusted off the snow, laughed it off, and adjusted their ski pants, something lingered with my mother: a persistent limp. "Oh, it's probably just a bit strained," she said. When we finally convinced her to at least take a break, she just brushed us off. Instead of seeing a doctor, she went to the hotel room, grabbed an ice gel pack for her knee—one of those truly nasty, rock-hard, ice-cold packs—and laid down in bed with it. No cloth. No protection. She just wanted to "rest for a moment." And, of course, she fell asleep.

When she woke up hours later, not only was her knee swollen, but her skin was burned. Ice crystals had literally dug into her leg. And now, whether she liked it or not, she had to go to the doctor. His diagnosis was one for the movies: torn medial ligament, torn lateral ligament, and second-degree burns from the ice pack. The doctor looked at her as if she were some combination of miracle and madness. "How were you even walking with that?" My mother just shrugged.

"Well, I thought I could still manage." She wasn't kidding. She genuinely believed that with two torn ligaments and ice burns, she could just "tough it out for a while."

But she's an Eckel. And Eckels don't quit. They power through on injured knees, laugh at ice burns, and when they wipe out a crowd of people with their skis, they at least do it with style.

Postscript: When we got home, the story naturally became a family legend. "Remember Mom and the ski trip?" "And how people fell like bowling pins?" "And then the whole thing with the ice pack?" My mother always laughed along and limped around for a while like a little everyday hero. But there was one thing she never did again: put an ice pack directly on her knee without a towel. Well, sometimes you learn the hard way. And sometimes all that's left afterward is laughter.

Tunisia: Camels, mosques, reporters, and the mishap on the escalator

When I was eighteen, we flew to Tunisia for a vacation at a Robinson Club. I imagined it as a sunny dream, but as is often the case with the Eckels, it turned into one of those trips where nothing went according to plan.

One day we visited a camel market, and suddenly my father found himself in the middle of a bizarre negotiation. A merchant approached us with an unbelievable offer: fourteen camels for me. At first, my father laughed, thinking it was a joke. But as the man became more and more insistent and other merchants started to gather around us, the situation quickly changed. The tone became serious. The merchant counted the camels as if they were gold bars, and my father realized the fun was over.

"Fourteen camels? For my daughter? What is this?" he asked, half-amused, half-annoyed. But the merchant kept pushing. The crowd pressed in closer, and the air grew thick. Completely bewildered, my father began to understand that this was no joke. The men stood right up to us, and I could see the tension rising. It became clear that we weren't just tourists at the market—this was something much more serious. The merchant was about to close the deal when my father, with a charming maneuver, smoothed things over and, through a mixture of diplomacy and sheer luck, got us out of the situation. When the men finally left, I felt a mixture of relief and shock. What would have happened if he had actually agreed? The thought of suddenly owning fourteen camels was almost as crazy as the rest of the vacation.

After this exciting incident, my mother, a friend, and I decided to visit a mosque. When we arrived, we were greeted by the same men from the camel market, and their demeanor was anything but friendly. They tried to pressure us again to go with them, but this time down a much narrower, darker path leading away from the mosque. We were completely confused and scared. What did they want from us? What would they have done if we hadn't reacted so quickly? Fortunately, the mosque supervisor appeared and quickly dealt with the men. He told them to leave us alone, providing the security we needed. We left the mosque fast, but this encounter definitely rattled us. Sometimes a harmless day in a foreign country can take an unexpected turn in an instant.

But the drama wasn't over yet. On the way back to the airport, as we walked through the terminal building, we were swarmed by reporters. The World Cup was on, and since my father was the legendary 1954 World Cup champion, everyone wanted his opinion on the current games. We tried to dodge the questions, but the reporters wouldn't leave us alone. The situation escalated, and eventually, airport authorities escorted us out of the terminal through a side entrance to escape the mob.

But another mishap was still to come. As we hurried through the back doors, disaster struck: my mother, completely exhausted from all the detours, stepped onto an escalator. Her clothes got caught. She couldn't free herself, and the escalator was shut down for several hours. Just another unwanted adventure that made this yet another Eckel vacation that was anything but ordinary.

Chaos in Cannes

It could have been so wonderful: summer, sun, and the French Riviera! I was seventeen or eighteen at the time, and my parents and I were traveling to Cannes. We had rented an apartment in a prime location. But within the first hour, fate had already decided: this was not going to be a relaxing vacation. It was going to be a stress test for our nerves. No sooner had we entered the apartment that evening than my mother had to call my grandmother to let her know we had arrived safely. Cell phones? No way—we were still living in the era of pay phones. So she went out, found one of those little devices in the hallway, and made the call. She put her big black purse on a shelf so she could have her hands free. Practical—except that she forgot it there.

When she returned shortly afterwards, the purse had—surprise, surprise!—disappeared. Inside it was everything: cash, checks, ID card-s—in short, our entire vacation fund. So there we were in Cannes, the epitome of luxury and glamour, with exactly zero francs in our pockets. And in the 1980s, you couldn't just transfer money—it took at least one or two days. If you were lucky. My father was—let's just say—less than thrilled. Mainly because he was hungry. And when dad was hungry, it wasn't just a physical need, it was a full-blown crisis. But without money, there was nothing we could do about it. The mood in the apartment was about as sunny as a storm over the Mediterranean. Dinner was canceled. Instead, we sat together like in a scene from a bad Hollywood movie: stranded, broke, and annoyed.

The next morning, my mother tried to organize some money. But as I said, we weren't yet living in the age of PayPal and instant transfers. The whole thing took a while. And the prospects for a relaxing vacation were rather bleak. An emotional storm was brewing. Just as we had resigned ourselves to living on baguettes for the rest of the week—the change was just enough for that—a surprise came: an honest person had turned in Mom's wallet! Thanks to the ID cards, it was returned to us via the apartment management. It was a small miracle! We had money again! Dad could finally eat—and I swear I've never seen anyone bite into a croissant with such devotion.

No sooner had the financial problem been solved than the universe apparently decided to present us with the next test.

Dad had confidently parked his Mercedes in the 'guarded' parking lot of the complex, much to mom's and my surprise, because every night car alarms were going off somewhere. One morning, the news came that several vehicles had been broken into. And which was the first victim? Of course—our Mercedes. The star? Torn off. The lock? Broken. Our vacation mood? Back in the basement. Dad took a deep breath, looked at the battered car, and said dryly, "I should have taken the Vwuptisch." That's what our family called Mom's VW Beetle. Even though his confidence had suffered a bit, he never lost his sense of humor. All the formalities, insurance stuff, reporting the crime—it all took a long time, especially with a tiny language barrier thrown in. Imagine a scene from a Louis de Funès movie: chaotic, loud, and somehow hilarious—only unfortunately, it was real.

But Cannes had even more surprises in store for us. A little trip to the casino was on the agenda. For me, however, it turned into an evening of "I'm standing around forever." We hadn't realized that at eighteen, I still wasn't allowed in. My parents went in; I stayed outside. For hours. It was a warm, starry night, romantic, but not for me. Especially not because of the imaginative pick-up lines of French men, which required neither imagination nor great language skills.

Another time, my parents went out in the evening and I stayed alone in the apartment. I had just made myself comfortable when I suddenly heard noises. Not pleasant noises, not the melodious baritone of a charming Frenchman from the neighboring apartment, but rather something like "Someone is trying to break down the door." I froze. I didn't breathe. I hoped I would just become invisible. After what felt like an eternity, the noises stopped, but the rest of the evening was ruined for me. I wavered between panic and hysteria. When my parents came home and I told them everything, Dad just said, "Great. First the money, then the car, now the apartment—the only thing missing is for us to break down on the way home, get towed, and end up at the police station."

That would have made a great headline—and this vacation truly unforgettable. Fortunately, it didn't come to that. But one thing was certain: this vacation had been nerve-wracking. Sun, sea, French flair? Yes, all that too. But above all, it was a week full of adventures that we would all have gladly done without. Conclusion: Cannes is beautiful. But next time, please without the typical Eckel chaos. Although—somehow, we can never quite do without it. At least it's never boring. "You don't go on vacation, you survive vacation—at least in our case."

New York: A handbag, a knife, and a lot of luck

New York. The city of lights, honking horns, steaming subway grates, and never-ending energy. My parents were visiting—without me—and had completely succumbed to the metropolis's charm. Marveling at skyscrapers, sampling bagels, racing through Manhattan in a yellow cab. That was the plan. But as always with the Eckels, the unpredictable was a constant companion on this vacation, because there, right in the middle of New York, it happened. Without warning. Without a soundtrack. Just like that.

My mother was walking down a busy street with a friend and my father when suddenly a man appeared out of nowhere and tried to snatch her handbag. No one shouted "Hands up!" There was no dramatic music, just a brutal tug on the strap, a hasty grab, and then a dash to escape. But the thief had done his equation without my father. While other men might have responded with a horrified cry or frantic waving, this incident triggered something completely different in him: his inner sportsman. And so he sprinted off. Without thinking. Without a plan. Without regard for previous warnings like, "If someone tries to rob you, for heaven's sake, DO NOT follow them into a side street." But that's exactly what my father did.

The thief turned into a dark, narrow alley. And my father—the family hero—followed him, unaware that he was walking straight into a trap. What awaited him was not only a damp brick wall but also the thief, who had pulled out a knife. A moment frozen in time. Breathing became shallow, the city outside continued its noise, but in this alley, everything was suddenly quiet—until help arrived. Acquaintances who happened to be nearby and two passersby, one of whom was probably a real New York guardian angel, came to his aid. They shouted something, they intervened, and the thief hesitated. He ran away. Without his loot, but also without consequences—like a shadow disappearing into the darkness.

My father returned, unharmed but pale. He said nothing. He sat quietly on a step, took a deep breath, and eventually said, "I know. I know. Side street. Knife. Not John Wayne." It was a moment that was almost symbolic in its mixture of stupidity, courage, and luck. Because anyone who knows my father knows he wasn't a daredevil. He was simply impulsive. And when someone attacked his wife, the teacher became the striker, and the walk turned into a chase.

Turkey: Blood, waves, and collective indifference

The sun shone warmly over the turquoise blue sea, I had the fine sand between my toes, and my five-year-old daughter squealed happily in anticipation of the water. It was a day straight out of a travel brochure: "Experience unforgettable moments with your loved ones!" Well, it was unforgettable. Just differently. Anna could swim, but not very well yet. So I picked her up, as I had done countless times before. She trusted me completely. Her small body pressed against mine, the salty water cooled our skin, and for a moment, the world was perfect. We walked in. Further and further, until the water reached our knees. Anna chattered happily while I kept my balance against the gentle, rolling waves. I was completely present with her, attentive, alert, and protective. Exactly as a mother is when she guides her child through life—in this case, literally carrying her.

Then came the moment that changed everything. I stepped on a rock with my right foot, or rather, my foot caught on it. The sea was like an unpredictable accomplice. At that very instant, it tugged at my leg, and my foot got stuck. I didn't hear anything, no snap, no scream, but I immediately sensed that something was terribly wrong. A sharp, blinding pain shot through my big toe. I looked down and saw blood! Not a small scratch. Not "Oh, it'll stop soon." No. It was pouring. It was running. It was flowing. Half of my toenail was ripped off. The sand clung to the open wound like salt in a fresh cut. I gritted my teeth. Not now. Not here. Not in front of my child. I still had Anna in my arms. She had noticed. "Mommy? Are you hurt?" she asked with that serious little face children make when they first realize that adults aren't invulnerable. I smiled, or at least I tried to.

"It's okay, sweetheart. Let's get out of the water." Walking. What an overly ambitious plan. Every step was torture. The waves kept coming, as if to test me: Let's see if she can still hold the child with the next blow. I fought my way forward. With a half-torn nail, a throbbing foot, and a five-year-old passenger on my hip. If someone had filmed me then, they might have thought it was a casting call for the next season of "Survivor." The beach was full of onlookers. And then came the sand. Oh, that beautiful, fine, cruel sand. I carefully put Anna down. She didn't want to let go, but I had to. I couldn't stand upright anymore. The pain stole my breath. I fell to my knees. And then—yes, really—I crawled. On my hands and elbows through the hot sand. My foot dragging behind me, like a warning: Remember your swim shoes next time. And all around me? People. People on towels, with sunglasses, magazines, drinks. People watching. People doing nothing. No one came. Not a single hand was offered. Not a single question was asked. They stared. Like at a traffic accident, where you hope the other person isn't really waving and saying, "Excuse me, could you help me for a moment?" I wasn't alone—but I couldn't have felt more isolated.

Somehow I made it to the hotel. A doctor was called. He came, looked, and said with a mixture of regret and medical determination: "Hospital." Once there, they laid me down on a stretcher. Anna was with me the whole time, like a little shadow that also brought light. The doctor examined my toe. "The nail has to go," he said matter-of-factly as if he were discussing a price tag. I nodded. They pulled it off. Then: rinse the wound, remove the sand. X-ray. Possibly broken. I lay there, exhausted, abandoned, in pain and salt water, thinking only one thing: I didn't let go of her.

Later, we sat outside. Me with a thickly bandaged foot, Anna with an ice cream that was more interested in her T-shirt than her mouth. She looked at me and asked, "Mama, is your foot still broken?" I laughed. "Yes. But you're okay, and that's the most important thing." Then she toasted me with her ice cream cone. I knew that everything was alright. Even though my toe still looks strange today, this moment is one I will never forget because I persevered. Because I carried her. Because, even in the bleeding, painful, sandy chaos, I was still a mother.

Of course, that's not the last of the Eckel chaos.

Contemplation with cowbells, gift crises, and the pug in the haystack

Holidays with the Eckel family. At first glance, that sounds like a cozy get-together, with fairy lights and the smell of cinnamon, cheerful singing, and loving hugs. Dream on. Our holidays were... let's just say... legendary. Not because they were so wonderful, but because they never went as planned. While other families smelled of pine branches and angelic patience, ours often reeked of frayed nerves, burnt goose, and dramatic performances with ironic endings.

Let's start with Christmas, the festival of love. For us, Christmas Eve traditionally began with an acoustic thunderclap: a cowbell. Not a dainty little bell. Not a glockenspiel app, but a full-blown, real, heavy cowbell that my parents had found somewhere. When it rang, my sister and I knew: It's go time! Time to unwrap the gifts. So we waited patiently outside the living room door, my sister usually a little skeptical, me eagerly anticipating it all like a Labrador waiting for a treat. Inside, of course, Grandma was already seated. She was always allowed to go in first. That was an unwritten law.

The door opened. The living room flickered in the candlelight, the tree was decorated (mostly crookedly, but with a lot of love), and a brass band version of something between "Silent Night" and "Jingle Bells" was playing on the record player. And then came my big task: I was allowed to hand out the presents. Every year. Always me. Why? Because I was the youngest and because I acted so seriously, like a ceremonial gift whisperer. But as soon as the wrapping paper rustled, the discord began. My mother was irritable and usually on the verge of a nervous breakdown because she had prepared the meal with my grandmother and had to endure at least three kitchen crises in the process. My father, who could never sit still, began his familiar ritual: pacing up and down. From the kitchen to the living room, from the living room to the balcony, from the balcony to the hallway—a kind of Christmas pendulum. My sister, who usually wanted to escape the hustle and bustle, eventually retreated to her room without a word. And I sat down on the carpet, looked at my presents, and sighed.

I was never a typical girl. While others adored dolls, I preferred to romp around outside, ride my bike through mud, read books, or swing from trees. But Christmas... it always brought on the same disaster. There it was again: the doll. Long blonde hair. Pink dress. And as a special feature: a record in its back. It sang. Yes! It sang "Der Mops im Haferstroh" (a German children's song about being happy as a clam). I swear, no child in the world wanted to hear that, unless they had an early affinity for folk curiosities. I stared at her. She stared back. Then she sang. All I could think was, "I'm adopted. This can't be my real present." A few days later, by the way, the doll had a new hairstyle. Very individual. Very asymmetrical. She still sang after that, but no one listened anymore.

Easter

Easter was also different for our family than for others. It began with a simple egg hunt in the garden. But our garden was no child's paradise; it was an obstacle course of thorny hedges, molehills, snail trails, and the occasional dog mess. Every egg was a risk. My father—the only man in the house, surrounded by girl power (including my grandmother, my mother, my sister, and our dog, Esther)—usually retreated to the sports field. That was his personal refuge. "Too much estrogen here," he would often say with a laugh. The rest of us struggled with chocolate bunnies, lamb-shaped cakes (that often looked more like broken dachshunds than lambs), and Grandma's mood, which always took a turn for the worse when she couldn't find the lemon flavoring again.

Birthdays—the open door to sensory overload

Birthdays were a completely different story. Not because of the cake or the candles, but because of the guests. Everyone was always welcome at our house. Seriously, everyone. My father was known for the fact that our front door was practically never closed on those days. "Come in! Make yourselves comfortable!" It didn't matter whether you were invited or not. This regularly led to a mix of friends, neighbors, distant relatives, and people who really just wanted to ask for directions.

It got loud. It got wild. Arguments, laughter, clinking glasses, slamming doors. And in the middle of it all: my grandmother. The calming influence. The patron saint of order. The woman who stoically stirred the dessert amid all the commotion until the moment she herself exploded. When Grandma had had enough, she became louder than everyone else combined. Her outbursts were legendary—short, sharp, and precise. After that, things usually quieted down again.

Conclusion: Harmony? Please. But unforgettable. Our holidays were never perfect. Never harmonious. Never "picture-perfect." But they were unique because we lived, argued, laughed, and celebrated wildly, and in the end, we were still together. And that's actually the best thing about the holidays.

A Single Heartbeat

It was a perfectly normal evening, but for all of us it could have been the end of our world as we knew it. One heartbeat, one second, and my perfect world would have ended in one fell swoop. The whole family, my parents and us children, were in the living room, and the TV was on. My mother and sister were sitting on the sofa, my father was in his armchair, and I was playing with building blocks at his feet. My grandmother was in her bedroom. She was not feeling well, as it was only a few days after the sudden death of my grandfather, Matthias Schey, from a heart attack. Perhaps this circumstance and the associated emotions, such as grief and shock, played a decisive role in the situation that now arose, because my mother was determined to hand over the rifle and pistol belonging to my grandfather, a former senior customs officer, to the relevant authorities as soon as possible. She was driven by the fear that the gun was still loaded and that there could be an accident. She talked to my father until he got up from his chair to get the pistol. He wanted to prove to my mother that the pistol was not loaded and that there was no reason for haste.

With the pistol in his hand, he sat back in his chair. He cocked the hammer and turned the drum, firm in his faith and trust in my grandfather, his father-in-law, whom he had loved like a father. The sentence Grandpa had said to him had probably been etched deep into his memory: "Horst, you don't need to worry, the guns aren't loaded." He pointed the pistol at my mother and pulled the trigger. "Click!" My mother flinched. Another "click" toward my sister and a third "click" as he held the revolver to his own temple. For some inexplicable reason, before pulling the trigger for the fourth time, he did not point the barrel of the revolver in my direction, as would have been logical, but upward toward the ceiling.

The deafening bang, accompanied by plaster splattering from the ceiling, was followed by a paralyzing silence that seemed almost unreal. Four pairs of eyes stared at the pistol, which my father held in his trembling hand for a brief moment before dropping it in dismay, as if it had burned him. It was one of those moments that can change a person's whole life. Horst Eckel, the once celebrated soccer world champion, husband, and family man who loved his wife and two daughters more than anything, came within a hair's breadth of shooting one of them. Of course, the weapon was removed from the house that same day.

The event had a profound effect on my father. Although he did regain his sense of humor at some point, another side of him was now more clearly evident. From then on, he was more serious, more thoughtful, and more level-headed in many ways. Qualities that shaped his future life as a family man, and also his career as a teacher. This event also had a lasting impact on me, but in a different way. My father had aimed at my mother, my sister, and himself. Why not at me? This question haunted me again and again into adulthood. But I just couldn't find an answer. I actually felt somehow left out. He had aimed and fired at every single member of the family, except me.

There is no rational explanation for what caused my father not to aim at me and pull the trigger. As I grew older, I asked him exactly that question: "Why didn't you aim at me?" He looked at me with his blue eyes, a look deep from his soul. "I don't know, my dear, but I thank God I didn't." On that memorable evening, fate had spared us. Why? I can't explain it. It probably wasn't meant to be. That one second, a heartbeat, could have ended my life.

Getting away with a black eye

There are stories that every family cherishes in its own way like a little treasure. They are told on birthdays, brought out on holidays, often with a glass of wine in hand and a smile on the lips, as if they have long been more a part of the family's inner inventory than any piece of furniture in the house. In our family, one of these stories begins with a robust little boy. And a dose of snake venom.

My father was not a delicate boy. On the contrary. He was a child who climbed trees, jumped in puddles, and never carried a handkerchief because he believed that the wind would take care of everything. He was strong, resilient, and sometimes a little stubborn. But even the strong are sometimes hit where it hurts and struck with full force by life. Even as a toddler, it is said, he suddenly became seriously ill. It started innocently enough—a slight fever, a little lethargy. But within a few days, his condition deteriorated dramatically. He just lay there, hardly drinking, refusing to eat. The family became increasingly nervous. The family doctor came, an old, experienced gentleman with a penchant for borderline treatment methods and a look that wasn't afraid of snakes. At some point, this doctor realized that the usual remedies weren't helping. Then he said something you wouldn't expect to hear in a German living room: "Let's try snake venom."

You can imagine my grandmother's face. The doctor stood there, looking serious, suggesting that a small, feverish child be given reptile venom. Not lethal, of course. In a tiny, carefully measured dose as an immune stimulant. "The body must learn to fight," he said. "Sometimes it needs an enemy to save itself." "Fifty-fifty," he added. My grandparents agreed. Not because they were convinced, but because they were desperate. There were no IVs, no machines. No white hospital walls, just a crib in the bedroom at home. And a little boy who, during those days, was somewhere between this world and the next without even knowing it. The poison was injected. And then they waited.

Two days later, the fever subsided. Three days later, he ate a few spoonfuls of soup. On the fourth day, according to the story that is still told today, he sat up, toddled into the living room, and asked, "Do you have any cookies?" In our family, that was the resurrection. No medical report, no file folder, no evidence. Just the memory: a little boy with a lion's heart, a doctor with snake venom, and a grandmother who probably never slept peacefully again when the doctor's visit lasted longer than five minutes. From then on, things went uphill, and not just in terms of health. My father grew up, became a teacher, became a family man—and above all, he became the person who later became the epitome of strength, stubbornness, and dry humor for us.

Decades later, when my father had long been working, something unusual happened. He suddenly developed extensive inflammation on his back—painful, uncomfortable, inexplicable. No dermatologist could figure it out, until a doctor, an elderly gentleman with a lot of experience, casually asked, "Have you ever had contact with snake venom?" My father, laconic as always, shrugged his shoulders and replied, "It saved my life once." Whether there was a connection was never clarified. But the idea that the snake venom was saying "hello, again" after all these years somehow fit into the story.

My father died in 2021. Although he is gone, his story remains. It lives on in conversations at the kitchen table, in family memories, in that absurd moment when a small child was saved by snake venom and, decades later, survived with a shrug, what would have knocked others down.

When we talk about it today, we laugh, not out of mockery, but out of awe, because he had often cheated life, grabbing it by the scruff of the neck when it threatened to slip away. And it all started with this crazy experiment, with a syringe full of venom and a family that had nothing but hope. Sometimes it doesn't take heroes, just a three-year-old with the courage of a lion, a few doctors with crazy ideas, and a family that says, "We'll try, because giving up is not an option."

How a champagne cork could change a life

There are moments when life doesn't scream loudly or intervene violently, but quietly cracks, pops, and clicks. A tiny moment, a casual impulse. A cork. A "pop." And suddenly everything hangs on it. One such moment was when my father almost lost his eyesight. He was traveling with his 1. FC Kaiserslautern teammates. The mood was relaxed, the game was behind them, and the drive home took them through the twilight. My father was sitting in the back of the car, and as so often, it was not the captain but a teammate who was at the wheel, because Fritz Walter, the great Fritz Walter, usually never drove himself. He had no interest in driving. And he was afraid of flying. But he was never averse to a glass of sparkling wine after a game.

That evening, he even had a bottle with him. At some point, he passed it over the back of the seat and said, "Horst, you open it. But watch out for the cork!" What happened next was not a soccer moment, it was a moment of destiny. The cork, hard and tense like a spring, came out with an ominous hiss—pop!—and shot with tremendous force straight into my father's eye. A noise. A cry. And then silence. Fritz commanded the car be stopped immediately, without discussion or hesitation. He leaned over to my father, looked at his eye, and made a decision without further ado: "We're going to the eye doctor right now."

The doctor took him in without waiting and looked and felt. He didn't write anything down, but said a sentence that cut through the room like a sword: "You will probably lose your eyesight." A single sentence that called everything into question. His whole life. His career. His dream. Everything now depended on one eye. My father could have lost himself in fear, anger, and self-pity at that moment. But he was not a man who gave up easily. And he was not alone. My mother took charge. With a calmness, a discipline, a quiet strength that cannot be learned, that is simply there when you need it.

She changed the bandages as instructed and followed every recommendation the doctor gave her . No daylight, no jolts, no exertion. Absolute rest. Absolute hope. And she didn't talk about fear, she talked about getting well. The crucial doctor's appointment was approaching. It was not a day like any other. My dad went in with mixed feelings—an inner mixture of hope and clarity. He knew that his whole life, as he had imagined it, could depend on this appointment. But he believed in himself and in the impossible. And he had my mother. No matter how it turned out, he knew that.

The treatment room fell silent. The doctor removed the bandage layer by layer. No sound, no comment. Then: a short sigh. Not one of resignation, but rather of assessment. Time seemed to stand still. Then he said, quietly, almost a little surprised: "Mr. Eckel… Your wife is an excellent nurse. You will keep your eyesight." My father didn't say much at that moment. But in his eyes—those famous, bright blue eyes—something flickered. He could see again. Not only with his eyes, but with his heart.

The cork could have meant the end. Instead, in retrospect, it almost became a touchstone. One of those breaking points where you see what really matters: trust. Closeness. And someone who not only treats your eye, but shows you what's to see. He returned to the field. Not immediately. Not without a detour. But he returned. And he saw clearly again. For a long time. A very long time. With a gaze that life itself had sharpened.

The voice that left and came back

It crept up slowly, as so often happens in life when something significant begins without you realizing it. In 1980, it was just a hint of hoarseness, a slight scratchy throat—the kind everyone gets from time to time. No one paid much attention to the symptom, least of all my father. But while we waited for it to get better, it only got worse. The hoarseness remained. And finally, he fell completely silent. The voice that had carried him through life—as a teacher, an athlete, a man of character and resonance—was suddenly gone. Without warning, without explanation.

The doctor finally diagnosed an infection. But not just any infection: the inflammation had attacked the nerves of his vocal cords and caused paralysis. Vocal cord paralysis—a technically cold term that didn't convey the impact it had on him and on us. The doctors couldn't say whether his voice would recover. There was no prognosis, no certainty. Only a new, oppressive silence. The change was enormous, not externally, but internally. My father was suddenly home, day after day. This was unusual, because he was normally out: at school, on the soccer field, at the tennis court, at events or clubs. A man on the move, now shut down. He settled in as best he could, and we did the same.

He placed a familiar, almost childlike object by his side: the large wooden Christmas cow with bells, which was otherwise only brought out when baby Jesus came on Christmas Eve. Now it served as his voice. Whenever he needed something, he rang the cow, and one of us came. Then he would quietly write a note, a request, a message, and we would do what needed to be done. A glass of water. A newspaper. A scarf. A quick look outside. That's how everyday life worked. Wordless, but not loveless. It was a quiet, strange time. And even though he was with us—more present than ever before—it felt as if part of him was somewhere else.

During this time, I often accompanied him to the hospital in Homburg. There, they tried to stimulate his paralyzed vocal cords with targeted electrical impulses. It was not an easy therapy. The sessions were unpleasant, and progress was barely measurable. And yet he kept going back—silent, but determined. We got used to the new silence. But behind the calm lay tension. None of us spoke openly about what we feared: that his voice might never return. And with it, perhaps, the person who was so deeply shaped by it.

Half a year passed. At some point, we quietly gave up hope. Not consciously, not dramatically, but rather insidiously, like the silence itself. We functioned as families do when words are not enough. But deep down, a question remained that no one asked: What if it stays this way? Then came that one day. My father cleared his throat. It was barely audible—like wind over dry leaves. But suddenly a word formed. A single word. Hoarse, barely intelligible, but unmistakable: a word. We held our breath. When a second word followed a moment later, something broke. The wall of uncertainty. The rigid, forced calm. The hope we had not allowed ourselves to have.

From that moment on, everything happened amazingly quickly. His voice returned, not immediately at full strength, but in steady steps. First came single words, then sentences, and finally the laughter we had missed for so long. He never told us how it had felt for him. Maybe he didn't want to look back. Perhaps silence was easier in this case. Or maybe it was just his way of processing things: by moving on, not by talking. But we knew how difficult this time had been, even if none of us ever said it out loud. We knew what was at stake. And we knew that with the loss of his voice, a part of his life could have been lost as well. If it hadn't come back, everything that came after—his work, his presence, his influence—would have been merely history. Or a different history. But it did come back. And with it, he came back.

The echo of illness: How history repeats itself

Some things repeat themselves without us understanding why. It isn't because they are planned. It isn't because anyone is to blame, but because life moves in cycles, sometimes with strange precision. I was three years old when my body suddenly gave out. It was as if fate had remembered that my father had been on the brink of death at exactly that age and decided to try again with me. A strange echo, an almost mirror image: a small child, a dark room, a body far too small for so much exhaustion. I, too, ended up in intensive care.

I don't remember much, but I remember exactly how it felt: like slowly disappearing, even though I was still right there. Like breathing was a mountain I had to climb over and over again. I remember how strange everything was—the machines, the harsh light, the voices that weren't speaking to me, but over me. I fought. And I stayed. Just like my father. Maybe it was just coincidence. Maybe something deeper. But looking back, it seems to me as if my life declared right at the beginning: "You will have to go through a lot. But you will persevere." And that is exactly what I did.

The daughter, the deer, and the hospital

The night was black as ink. No stars in the sky, no noise from outside, the window was just a dark spot in the room. Something I didn't know or understand was raging inside my little body, slowly silencing me. I was three years old. And very, very sick. Not the "I have a stomach ache" kind of sickness. Not the kind that gets better with warm tea and a goodnight kiss. It was different. Deeper. More threatening. My body was exhausted. I was tired of breathing. My mother sensed that something was wrong. She sat by my bed, held my hand, and ran her fingers over my forehead.

As if she were searching for something only she could see. "We have to go," she said quietly in that voice no child wants to hear because it tells you: Now it's serious. My father came into the room. Without saying much. He picked me up and wrapped me in a blanket. I smelled his jacket, the aftershave that usually made me feel safe but wasn't enough this time. I heard my mother grab her bag and rush down the hall. Then the front door closed behind us.

The car was cold. The engine didn't start right away. When it finally did, the world outside was still dark. We drove off. I lay in the back seat, wrapped up, silent. Too weak to speak. But then, suddenly, a bright flash—and a dull thud. A deer. A real deer, in the middle of the night, on the road. It was like slow motion. The headlights caught its face, its tense muscles as it leaped, then a hard blow. The car swayed. My father cursed. My mother held her breath. I opened my eyes. Not much, but enough to sense that this was no normal evening. We drove on, had to drive on. Because of me. The deer was gone. No one ever told me for sure whether it survived. But in my childish heart, I felt that it was like me. Overwhelmed, hurt, taken by surprise.

For adults, a hospital may be a place with rules, plans, and systems. For me, it was a labyrinth of cold light, beeping machines, and unfamiliar faces. Everything was too bright, too big, too fast. I was taken to the intensive care unit. A word I didn't know at the time, but I felt it. They pushed me into a white bed with bars. Cables were connected. Voices took turns. No one spoke to me, everyone talked about me. But where was mom? I looked around. I thought: She'll be here soon. She'll definitely be here soon. But she didn't come. A nurse—friendly, firm—said my mother couldn't stay. "This is important for you right now," she said. But my heart didn't want to hear it. I clung to the fabric of her jacket, the last remnant of home I still had.

Then she was gone. I lay there—small, sick, alone. The night grew lighter, but not warmer. I didn't eat anything. I didn't say anything. I was there, but not really. The days passed. Or hours. I don't know. Time meant nothing there. I refused everything. Food, drink, closeness. The nurses smiled, asked me, tempted me with dolls or juice, but I just stared at the door. I knew that everything would be fine once my mother came back. She was fighting outside, I learned later. She tried to see me again, but the rules were strict. Too strict.

The doctor finally took her into a small room, placed a glass of water on the table that no one drank, and said calmly but firmly, "Your daughter refuses everything. And I wonder, Mrs. Eckel... how is a child who is attached to only one person supposed to survive? You have bound her very closely to you." My mother said nothing. "What if something happens to you? What will your daughter do then? She has to learn to be on her own. Let go, Mrs. Eckel. You have to let her go." My mother, as I know her, took a deep breath. Then she looked up, very calmly. And said, "I'll let her go when she's healthy again. Not before."

When she finally came back to me—in one of those rare, far too short visiting hours—the hospital suddenly became quieter. She sat down next to me, put her hand on mine, and said nothing. She didn't need to say anything. Her closeness was everything. I started to eat. Slowly. Suspiciously. But I ate. And I began to return to myself. To my body. To my laughter. This story was often told in our family. A little romanticized, sometimes smiled at. "Oh, you and your drama at three," they said. But I know it was more than that. It was the moment I learned how strong the bond between mother and child can be. Not because you feel it, but because you need it. Because it's there when nothing else helps. And maybe the deer that night was a harbinger. A sign that something was about to break. But in the end, I stayed. And so did she.

The long shadow: When the illness returned

It happened again, differently this time—a different age, new means—yet it felt so familiar I could hardly believe it. I was in my late twenties, in the middle of my life, in the process of building something, of becoming. And suddenly, it arrived: this invisible enemy, a virus I knew nothing about, uninvited, but permanent. Not for weeks. Not for months, but for years. At first, it was just weakness. Fatigue. A feeling as if someone were quietly draining my strength. But then, days of discomfort turned into a chronic condition. A life lived in the shadows.

I didn't understand what was happening. Doctors couldn't find a clear cause. Sometimes there was hope, sometimes utter helplessness. I went through therapies, diagnoses, and doubts. My body simply stopped cooperating. My mind wanted to, but couldn't. Three years of my life were enveloped in a kind of fog, not just physically, but emotionally, too. I was still present, but it was like looking through a pane of glass. I watched life pass me by. Friends, plans, dreams—everything seemed to move forward, while only I stood still. Or was swept away in a direction I didn't recognize. From the outside, it was difficult to see. An invisible illness quickly becomes a question of credibility. Sometimes I asked myself: How long can I endure this without losing myself completely? It wasn't just a battle against a virus. It was a battle for my identity. For my energy. For myself.

This state lasted until 2010. It was a tough, dark river from which I could only slowly pull myself back to shore. Step by step. Day by day. It wasn't a dramatic turning point or a moment of sudden relief, but a gradual reawakening. I began to breathe again and feel what was important to me, to fight—not with my fists, but with patience. With dedication. With a quiet anger that declared, "I want to come back." And I did come back. Not as the same person. But as someone who knows what it feels like when everything hangs in the balance. Perhaps it wasn't a coincidence. Maybe it was part of that invisible connection that linked me to my father. Like me, he had fought for his life at the age of three. And he, too, had later returned from silence—with a voice, with conviction, with new clarity.

Seen in this light, my illness was not merely a repetition. It was part of history. A chapter that hurt, but one that showed me that life goes on, even when you doubt it for a long time. As I mentioned earlier, there were many situations in our family that seemed dramatic at first glance and sometimes foreshadowed something terrible, but in the end, almost everything turned out well. My father was particularly affected by such events in his sporting career. It started very early on. His coach at 1. FC Kaiserslautern, Richard Schneider, and especially his great role model and later fatherly friend and mentor, Fritz Walter, who was twelve years his senior, predicted that he would one day play for the national team. But my father couldn't imagine that at all. Fritz Walter's great skills had always impressed him deeply. Playing with him on the same team at 1. FC Kaiserslautern was already the fulfillment of a big dream. But then to be called up to the national team by national coach Sepp Herberger… no, that felt too away…

Why my father forgave his white lie

And yet it happened. My father was just twenty years old when he had to play with Kaiserslautern against TuRa Ludwigshafen. Before the game, Fritz Walter came up to him and said, "Horst, the boss is here today—the national coach. He wants to see you play. So just play your game." The match went very well for my dad; he even scored two goals, but a few minutes before the end of the game, he was fouled, fell, and broke the little finger on his right hand. He knew immediately what had happened, and when Fritz Walter asked him on the way to the locker room what was wrong with his finger, my father answered truthfully that it was broken.

Fritz Walter immediately disagreed with my father and insisted that the finger was surely just sprained. But my father was certain that the finger was broken. Fritz Walter just shook his head and told my father that Sepp Herberger would be coming to the dressing room to inform him that he had been nominated for the upcoming international match against France in Paris. Therefore, if the boss asked about his injury, he should tell him that his finger was sprained.

And, of course, Sepp Herberger asked what injury my father had sustained. Although my father, as he later described, struggled internally and wanted to tell the truth out of enormous respect for the national coach, he nevertheless replied, because he felt Fritz Walter's gaze on him: "It's just a sprain, Mr. Herberger."

I can well imagine my father's inner struggle. National coach Herberger was a person he respected immensely. Lying to his boss was very difficult for him, but since Fritz Walter had advised him to do so, he overcame his reservations, because Fritz Walter meant everything to my father. When Sepp Herberger told him after this brief conversation in the locker room that he would be playing in the next international match, my father quickly forgave himself for his little "white lie."

Even though the situation in the locker room must have been very uncomfortable for my father—because he couldn't tell Sepp Herberger the truth without fearing that he would not be nominated for the upcoming international match due to his injury—he was also ambitious enough to do everything he could to be selected by Herberger. He took soccer very seriously, and it's safe to assume that these qualities were the reasons why Sepp Herberger made my dad a national team player.

Sepp Herberger probably already knew that it wasn't just a sprain. "The boss knows everything"—my father knew that, and all the national players knew that. But he also turned a blind eye to some things, always in such a way that his players were confident that he was aware of what was going on. During the preparatory training camp before the World Cup in Switzerland, after training, a few players were standing around in the dining room with cups of drinks whose contents could not be identified. Herberger came over and immediately realized from the reaction of his players that some of them were probably enjoying a beer. "Guys, what you're doing isn't good," he said reproachfully, looking with satisfaction at some embarrassed faces. "It's not good, guys, to drink cold milk like that in the evening."

With these words, he left the players alone again, and most of them actually poured out the rest of their beers. My father, however, had actually only been drinking milk. He didn't like alcohol at all, and he couldn't tolerate it either. It is all the more ironic that it was he, the teetotaler, who almost lost his eyesight when a champagne cork shot out of the bottle. As bad as this accident was, it could have ended much worse. A few years later, however, an event occurred that could have been even more dramatic and frightening.

Another such example, and perhaps the most significant in my father's soccer career, was the serious injury he sustained in the final in Bern, shortly before the end of the first half, in a tackle with Hungary's Mihály Lantos: a deep, 20-centimeter-long laceration that needed stitches. But substitutions were not allowed at that time, and continuing to play with one man down would have meant certain defeat against the favored Hungarian team. Horst Eckel, my father, dutiful and ambitious as ever, refused medical treatment. "I can't just leave the others on their own..." He had his leg bandaged, gritted his teeth, and continued playing. An hour later, Germany was world champion.

More Than Mentors: The Men Behind My Father

Fritz Walter and Sepp Herberger were the two men who not only gave a significant boost to my father's soccer career, but also profoundly influenced him as a person. All three came from humble backgrounds, and despite their different personalities, they shared key characteristics: ambition, discipline, and, above all, a passion for soccer.

I was present a few times when Sepp Herberger and my father met, but I don't have any clear memories of those encounters; I wasn't even nine years old when Herberger died. Nevertheless, I know a lot about him from my father's stories and from my own extensive reading.

My father's bookcase held quite a bit of literature on Sepp Herberger. He was born in Mannheim in 1897, when Germany was still an empire. His father had found work at the Saint-Gobain mirror factory in the Waldhof district. This allowed the family to move into a company apartment directly opposite the factory, in what was known as the "mirror colony." As a good student, young Josef—his birth name, which hardly anyone used—was permitted to transfer to the Bürgerschule (a type of pre-secondary school), but he had to leave just one year later when his father died at age 53. With his father's death, the right to the company apartment automatically expired. Furthermore, Sepp Herberger's mother could no longer afford the tuition required for the Bürgerschule.

When I accompanied my father to Waldhof in April 2015 for the groundbreaking ceremony of the planned Sepp-Herberger-Platz, and later for the square's inauguration directly in front of the former national coach's elementary school, I learned many interesting things about Sepp Herberger's childhood and youth from the accounts of people who knew him. Little "Seppl" had gotten involved with soccer early on, having previously been a very good gymnast. At first, the children in Waldhof played soccer in the streets or in open spaces between the houses and played "Kellerlöchels" (cellar holes), as one of his former friends explained, because the openings of the cellar windows served as goals. In 1907, SV Waldhof was founded, and Sepp Herberger joined a few years later. From then on, soccer dominated his life.

Sepp Herberger on his way to the top

Through hard work in training and natural skill, Sepp Herberger made it onto SV Waldhof's first team at the age of 16 and quickly became a regular starter. In 1921, he received his first nomination for the German national team and rapidly developed into one of Germany's top strikers. But even then, Herberger was already thinking ahead. In 1925, while still an active player, he enrolled in a coaching course at the Deutsche Hochschule für Leibesübungen in Berlin (German College of Physical Education in Berlin). There, he caught the attention of the college's director, Carl Diem, who was impressed by his performance and, considering him "particularly gifted," offered him a spot in the course under a special exception since Herberger did not have a high school diploma.

Sepp Herberger pursued his career with determination and the same meticulousness he would later use as a coach, not only preparing for upcoming games but also tailoring the role of each player to the specific opponent. In 1932, when he received an offer to become a sports instructor for the Westdeutscher Spiel-Verband (West German Sports Association, the association for soccer and athletics), he jumped at the chance. The role involved not only developing young talent but also promoting top athletes, which allowed Sepp Herberger to work alongside Otto Nerz, the national soccer team coach at the time.

In addition to his professional skills, Herberger was characterized by considerable ambition, to which he subordinated many other things. After the National Socialists took over the government in March 1933, he joined the NSDAP shortly thereafter, but only to continue his work, not out of political conviction. Sepp Herberger had basically no interest in politics. Soon after, the regional associations were dissolved and merged into the Deutscher Reichsbund für Leibesübungen (German Reich Sports Federation). From that point on, Sepp Herberger served as Otto Nerz's assistant and succeeded him as Reich Coach in 1936.

When World War II broke out, Sepp Herberger fought with all his energy to exempt his players from frontline service for as long as possible. He organized training courses and continued to arrange international matches until 1942. Nevertheless, he remained in contact with each player even after that, writing countless letters during this time, and became deeply concerned when he did not receive a reply from one of them for a long time. In September 1944, he was even drafted himself, but only for a few days before being discharged for health reasons. All biographers emphasize that after the war's end, Sepp Herberger fought for his denazification with the same energy he had shown in fighting for his players during the war, all so he could organize the rebuilding of the national team. Even before the German Football Association was re-established, he reportedly gave lectures as a soccer instructor at the Sports University in Cologne and soon after resumed training courses for national players at the Duisburg-Wedau Sports School, his old workplace. He also temporarily took over coaching at several clubs in the Oberliga (upper league). However, these were only temporary positions. His main goal was the national team, which would become his life's work. On January 21, 1950, the German Football Association was finally re-established. One month later, Sepp Herberger was officially appointed national coach. The rebuilding of the German national team could begin.

A key player in Sepp Herberger's plans was Fritz Walter, alongside whom my father played at 1. FC Kaiserslautern and under whose mentorship he became a national player. Fritz Walter had played his last international match eight years earlier and was now almost 30 years old. That was one consideration. The other was Fritz Walter's exceptional talent, which my father always spoke of in the highest terms. It was often said that Fritz Walter had already amazed adults as a seven-year-old boy playing on the school team. Even at a young age, he could do everything with the ball, learned to read and control the game as he matured, and was also a feared goal scorer.

Above all, he was able to implement tactical instructions during a game. In this way, Fritz Walter increasingly became Sepp Herberger's right-hand man on the field. The war had robbed him of many peak years as a soccer player, but his best years were yet to come. At least, that was the firm conviction of Sepp Herberger, who consequently appointed him team captain.

Fritz Walter himself was far less convinced of his abilities than "the boss." He was a highly sensitive person who, despite all his skills, was constantly plagued by self-doubt. Everyone who played with him for a long time knew this. He often had to be cheered up and motivated by his teammates, especially his brother Ottmar, sometimes in a somewhat harsh manner and with strong words, as my father reported. Fritz Walter tended to blame himself for a bad game. This went so far that he asked Sepp Herberger not to select him anymore after Germany lost 3-1 to France in Paris in October 1952 and he, like the rest of the team, had performed unexpectedly poorly.

But Sepp Herberger rejected all of Fritz Walter's arguments and stood by him. He needed him for the 1954 World Cup. The qualifying matches were just around the corner. With psychological skill, the boss consistently built up his most important player. Sepp Herberger, who had no children of his own, treated Fritz Walter like his own son. He cheered him on when he was depressed after defeats and talked about his strengths when he had played well. The two trusted each other implicitly. Fritz Walter knew that when the boss said something, it was true, and Herberger knew that Fritz would execute his strategy to the letter.

Fritz Walter: From idol to mentor and friend

Just as Sepp Herberger was a father figure to Fritz Walter, years later Fritz Walter became a father figure and mentor to my own father. When Fritz Walter played his last international match before he went to war in 1942, my father was just ten years old. Fritz Walter was already a legend when my father first kicked a ball. But my father had the ambition that Sepp Herberger also possessed and wanted in his players, along with the discipline necessary to achieve great things. What's more, my father was just as obsessed with soccer as "the boss" and Fritz Walter. These three men were destined to meet eventually.

In 1949, at the age of 17, my father moved from SC Vogelbach to 1. FC Kaiserslautern, making the leap from a small village club to one of Germany's top soccer clubs. A year earlier, he had seen Fritz Walter play for the first time in a friendly match. He and a friend had cycled the 30 kilometers from Vogelbach to Kaiserslautern. Once there, they crawled under the fence at the Betzenberg stadium because they couldn't afford admission. What my father saw initially left him more discouraged than excited. While my father was one of the best players on the SC Vogelbach team, he could now see firsthand how good "real" soccer players were. Fritz Walter was the player who impressed my father the most.

"He controlled the game and passed balls left and right to the wing positions. He was everywhere on the pitch, always available for a pass, and he scored goals," my father often recounted in interviews when asked about Fritz Walter. "He could do that with both his left and right foot. I had never seen anything like it before. Fritz Walter was a true soccer player." The profound impression that my father had to process after seeing Fritz Walter play in person only motivated him to train even more relentlessly.

A year later, my father was playing for the same club as the great Fritz Walter, though initially on the youth team. But that didn't last long. Just one year after my father moved from SC Vogelbach to 1. FC Kaiserslautern, he was playing alongside Fritz Walter on the first team and was now part of the "Walter XI," as the Kaiserslautern team was known.

For my father, a major dream had come true, and he knew who deserved the credit. Fritz Walter, who himself always needed encouragement from "the boss," supported the young Horst Eckel whenever necessary. He motivated him, cheered him on, but also criticized him when needed, and offered helpful advice. Just as Fritz Walter tried to implement the boss's instructions and tactics, my father followed Fritz Walter's advice. Fritz Walter was more convinced of my father's strengths than my father was himself at the start of his time at 1. FC Kaiserslautern. But as he developed more and more skills through hard work and discipline in training, his self-confidence also grew. His mental toughness was a quality that even surpassed that of his great role model.

What my father couldn't have known at the time was that the national coach also saw something in my father that he himself was not yet aware of. When they first met, Sepp Herberger not only saw that my father's finger was in fact broken, not just sprained. He also saw that my father was determined to travel to Paris for the international match, and knew that Fritz Walter wanted him there.

My father was indeed about to make his first international appearance, but initially, he was only sitting on the bench in Paris. The German team was struggling, and with the score tied at 1-1, Sepp Herberger instructed my father to warm up. Shortly afterward, France took a 2-1 lead, and the national coach signaled that the substitution would not be made after all and that my father should return to the bench. Shortly before the end of the game, France scored again to make it 3-1. It was the game after which Fritz Walter had wanted to end his career. Of course, my father was disappointed that he hadn't made his international debut, but he quickly realized that the national coach had only wanted to protect him. My father was the youngest player in the squad and had not yet played in an international match. Sepp Herberger didn't want to put him into a game that was going poorly and would most likely end in defeat.

If my father had been called into action, he probably would have dwelled on that defeat for a long time. But as it happened, he was able to go into the next game, which took place just a month later in Augsburg against Switzerland, with a clear head. My father played from the start, and Germany won 5-1. Now my father was truly a national team player.

But being a national team player was one thing; being truly accepted into the inner circle of national players was quite another. There was an initiation ritual that every new national player had to endure: he received the "Blessing of the Holy Spirit." This involved the newcomer having his pants pulled down and walking through the ranks of his teammates, who each gave him a hard slap on the butt. Only those who proved themselves to be "real men" in this way were worthy of becoming members of this special group.

As my father later recalled, it took a very long time for him to receive the Holy Spirit, and he felt he had been overlooked. However, there was a very plausible reason for this. Horst Eckel, "the Greyhound," seemed to consist only of skin and bones—very hard bones, as everyone who had ever tackled him knew. Therefore, each of his teammates feared that the ritual would cause them more pain than my father himself. But eventually, the time came, the Holy Spirit was administered, and my father finally belonged to the national team.

Although Fritz Walter and my father were initially teammates, over time their interpersonal relationship grew closer and developed into a deep and lifelong friendship. In earlier years, Fritz Walter was Sepp Herberger's protégé, but later a father-son relationship developed between Fritz Walter and my father. When Fritz Walter married his wife Italia in 1948, Sepp Herberger was, of course, his best man. When my father married his Hannelore in 1957, it was clear from the outset that only Fritz Walter would do as his best man.

"What would I be without you?"

My father always insisted that he owed everything to Fritz Walter, believing he would be nothing without him. This conviction stemmed from an almost excessive respect for his great idol. However, Fritz Walter would often ask his teammates the same rhetorical question with equal sincerity and conviction: "What would I be without you?" As a brilliant playmaker, he required the security and certainty that "nothing would go wrong at the back" so he could play freely up front. Fritz Walter knew he could rely on my father. Sepp Herberger knew it too.

When my father was assigned a task, he committed to it, regardless of how the game unfolded. This was especially evident in the Bern final. While Fritz Walter directed the German team's offense, my father successfully neutralized the Hungarian team's playmaker, Nandor Hidegkuti, preventing him from developing their game. Sepp Herberger was not the only one who considered this a key to the victory. Just as the seasoned Fritz Walter supported the young Horst Eckel at the start of his career, my father supported Fritz Walter, whose health was failing at the end of his life. He accompanied him to appointments, and only my father was allowed to push the wheelchair that Fritz Walter depended on in his final years.

The values that Sepp Herberger and Fritz Walter had modeled for my father—diligence, discipline, loyalty, and ambition—were fully embraced by him. He, in turn, passed them on to his children and later, as a teacher, to his students. He once proudly shared the story of a former student who confessed to him many years after graduating: “Mr. Eckel, when you used to lecture us about diligence, discipline, and loyalty, we sometimes made fun of it. But today, I can say you were absolutely right about everything, and I am passing on what you taught us back then to my own children.”

Incidentally, one of his students at the secondary school in Kusel was Miroslav Klose, who later played for 1. FC Kaiserslautern and, sixty years after my father, also became a world champion. The two met often, and Miro often stressed how much my father had influenced him. These belated acknowledgments from his former students meant a great deal to my dad; they were not only a confirmation of his work but also a continuation of the legacy of Fritz Walter and Sepp Herberger.

Dark Moments

Dark moments have been part of my life from the very beginning. It wasn't all good times, as many outsiders might think—as if I were living in a fairy tale. Even before I could enter the so-called glittering world, I had to learn about the darkest parts of human nature.

It started when I was seven years old. Like any other day, I was walking home from elementary school in Vogelbach, where I attended first and second grade. My route took me along a narrow path with a few steps—the playground on the right, bushes on the left. Suddenly, four boys jumped out of the bushes. I knew them; they were a grade above me and lived in the same village. Without a word, they grabbed me and dragged me into the bushes. One held me down while the others kissed and touched me one after the other. It was hell. I didn't know what was happening or why. I was just helpless—powerless. That feeling of helplessness was worse than anything else.

When they finally let me go, I ran home, crying. My mother was there. She listened to me, let me explain everything, and took immediate action. She went to school, spoke to my teacher, who personally walked me home for the next eight days. She also spoke to the boys' families. But I still couldn't forget it. I couldn't process it, at least not as a child. When I asked my mother why something like this happened, she said, "You have to understand. These boys come from difficult backgrounds. You have to have compassion for them, forgive them." So I tried. Nevertheless, for a long time, it was almost unbearable for me to encounter these boys every day at school or in our village. They didn't leave me alone after this incident. Quite the opposite. In the summer, at the outdoor pool, they kept trying to get close to me and sometimes even laid down on my blanket. Their threatening behavior intimidated me every time. But I couldn't do anything about it. According to my mother, it wasn't their fault, and I should forgive their behavior. I tried to act normal and be nice to them because I thought that was the right thing to do. I understood that they had less than I did and I knew that they came from different social backgrounds. I believed that they didn't mean me any harm because they actually liked me. I was always friendly and polite, as my mother had taught me to be.

But today I know that this was no reason to forgive, to remain silent, and to ignore my own feelings. I was a child, and I was hurt. I am allowed to acknowledge this and do not have to make excuses for anything that hurt me. Instead, I can say, "That was wrong."

This experience shaped me. It laid the foundation for me to forgive many people who also hurt me later in life. I thought that was the right way to live—forgive, understand, apologize. But that's not always right, because if you constantly forgive, you eventually lose sight of your own rights—the right not to be hurt. Today, I know that I don't have to forgive just because someone expects me to. I don't owe understanding to anyone who has hurt me. I only owe the little child inside me protection, dignity, and healing.

A Strong Mother's Heart

It was a cold winter morning when the teachers sent me home. I was feeling weak and miserable so they decided that I should go. Just eight years old, in the third grade, I didn't know that this day would bring me more than just another end of a schoolday. The streets were almost empty, the fog hung heavy in the air, and the world was enveloped in an oppressive silence. I lived in Vogelbach, but my school was in Bruchmühlbach. I had to stop at the phone booth to call my mother to pick me up. It was no big deal. I went to the phone booth, picked up the phone, and talked to my mother. Nothing seemed unusual.

As soon as my mother hung up the phone, she knew that every second counted. It was just a stone's throw between Vogelbach and our village, barely a two-minute drive, but anything could happen in those two minutes. The police had warned her that we were being watched. And because I was the weakest link, it was assumed that I was to be the victim.

To my mother, at that moment, it was no longer a mere assumption, but a certainty. She knew exactly what could happen if she didn't act immediately. It was a race against time. Without hesitation, she grabbed the car keys, tore open the door, and ran outside. The engine roared, the tires screeched, and she drove off—faster than she had ever driven before. In her head, only a single, inexorable thought: My daughter's life depends on it. I have to make it before it's too late.

When I ended the conversation and left the phone booth, the world suddenly felt different. Something menacing hung in the darkness of the morning, and the air around me suddenly seemed to thicken. A strange feeling came over me, as if I were no longer alone. Something did not feel right. Something was watching me, but I couldn't name it.

Suddenly, I heard the sound of a car. The white car was suddenly there, without warning. It stopped right next to me. I couldn't react, stood on the sidewalk as if paralyzed. The driver opened the door, and before I knew what was happening, he grabbed me. His grip was hard, relentless, a feeling I will never forget. I wanted to scream, wanted to run away, but I was trapped. As if in slow motion, he pulled me into the car. My body froze. I couldn't do anything. The cold of the car enveloped me as the man pulled me into the car. The shock paralyzed me. I couldn't even cry. My heart raced, my thoughts whirled, but my body remained rigid, unable to act. A cold, almost lifeless state.

And then, out of nowhere, a loud honking broke the silence. It was my mother's car! She sped toward the white car with a roar, and the man flinched. Without another word, he pushed me out of the car. I stumbled, but managed to catch myself. The shock hit me like a blow. I stood there stunned. My heart was pounding so loudly that I could hear it in my ears. All I could do was stand, rigid, as the world around me went on in slow motion. But then my mother jumped out of her car. Her eyes searched for me, found me, and she pulled me tightly into her arms. She didn't say a word, but I read everything in her eyes—the fear, the relief, the love. She had saved me. She had reacted in time. At the time, I didn't really understand what had happened. I knew it was dangerous, but I didn't feel any fear. My mother was there; that was all that mattered. She wrapped her arms around me, and for me, the world was right again. I was safe again. My mother never talked about it. She didn't want to burden me with this fear, and she didn't want to draw me into the world of the media and the public at that young age. She wanted to protect me from the additional pressure. That's why there was no police complaint, at least none that I knew about. Maybe she had gone to the police, maybe she had filed a report, but she never told me. I can imagine that she did though. Firstly, she suspected that there was more to this incident than met the eye, and secondly, she wanted to ensure that other children would not have to suffer the same fate. She wanted to protect others from a similar disaster.

Years later, my mother told me that someone had been watching us for a while. Especially me, as the youngest, the "easiest target." She knew I was in danger. She had noticed it, had recognized the signs, and was there at the right moment. But I wasn't aware of that at the time. All I knew was that she had saved me. But this incident left its mark. A feeling of not being safe that never subsided. This queasy feeling that something could happen, that someone out there was waiting to do something to me. Unfortunately, this wasn't the first time I had found myself in such danger. But there was always a protective hand that saved me.

Perhaps it was this event that sharpened my senses. Perhaps from that moment on, I learned to recognize dangers more quickly and to protect myself from them. It was a lesson that life taught me. As a child, I didn't understand the extent of what I had experienced. It wasn't until

I got older that I realized how close I was to danger. But back then, only one thing mattered to me. My mother had saved me. In her arms, everything felt safe again. This feeling of safety she gave me, I carried with me as if it were the only truth.

Sitting on a Segregated Bus

I was in a new chapter in my life that challenged me for the first time in a way I never expected. At the end of the 1970s, we were in Miami to visit some friends. The sun was shining, and as always, my skin was tanning quickly. The slightly darker skin color comes from my mother's side of the family. My grandfather was very dark, and my mother always said that it had even skipped several generations and was particularly evident in me. It was always a special story in my family when they talked about my birth, I was brown and hairy all over. That's why my sister also thought I was a little monkey. Thank God the fluff disappeared after a few days. So for me it was completely normal. But what was natural for me became a "label" for others, marking me as "different." My parents always taught me that there were no differences between people—regardless of their skin color, religion, or background. But on that day, I had to learn that these values and the right to humanity did not apply equally to all people. I was out with one of the family's sons, and we wanted to take the bus to a playground. In my childish naivety, I didn't notice the people who got on at the front or back of the bus and that there was a difference. However, the bus driver blocked my way. He kept explaining to me that I had to get in the back. Since my English wasn't very good yet, I didn't understand him right away. But at some point, I realized that I should get in the back.

It was only when I sat down that I noticed the silence around me. No one spoke to me. No one explained to me what was going on. The people who sat with me in the back of the bus were very quiet and reserved, introverted. Only occasionally did a glance meet me from beneath half-closed eyelids. It was as if they lived in their own world, as if they were afraid to deal with me. Every now and then, very occasionally, I was met with a smile—nothing more than a friendly but ghostly sign of understanding or pity. The atmosphere was filled with an oppressive silence that overwhelmed me emotionally. I felt isolated and excluded, as if I were in a strange world that I didn't understand.

Then it suddenly dawned on me: The bus was "segregated." People who were considered "white" in society sat at the front, and people who were considered "non-white" sat at the back. And I was sitting in the back of the bus. I had never had to think about my skin color or its shade. But now I became painfully aware that this separation based on skin color existed and that I suddenly belonged to those who were considered "different." However, belonging to a group of people who were seen as different actually made me feel strong. However, it was something else entirely that truly affected me— I was shocked by the indifference of the people on the bus. It wasn't just a segregation, it was the habituation, the acceptance, and the indifference that was deeply ingrained in the minds of many. How naturally this separation, this unequal treatment of people, was considered "normal."

I don't know exactly what was really going on in these people's hearts, but outwardly, all strength and resistance seemed to have been lost. And although I didn't know or understand much about it at the time, I sensed that something unfair, something incomprehensible, was going on. I knew that it used to be much worse many years before. People had fought in the streets, protested, given speeches, and given their lives for human rights. Men and women such as Martin Luther King Jr., Rosa Parks, and many others dedicated themselves and their lives to ending the unjust systems of racial segregation and discrimination.

Why did it feel like nothing had really changed? Why was I still sitting in the back of the bus, even though so many people had fought for the freedom that I and everyone else on that bus should have had? I didn't understand why this injustice just kept happening. How long would it take for the truth to penetrate people's hearts and for them to understand? Had the many struggles and sacrifices really changed nothing? I was literally sitting between two worlds. I didn't really belong to either of these worlds and didn't want to. But at that moment, in the silence between all these people with their prejudices and fears, I realized for the first time that I had been trapped between two worlds for a long time.

Here, it was my skin color that made me "different," but in everyday life, it was my name and the heritage associated with it. This name that distinguished me from the others from the very beginning. I had never been "normal" or "average." Something had always set me apart from the others. From the very beginning, my name was a characteristic that set me apart from the general public. This realization hurt. I understood that I had never been simply "neutral" to others. A fact that I had always sensed unconsciously and that I was also made to feel. I was judged and pigeonholed, never to escape.

But there was one thing they could never take away from me—my love for my father and the pride I felt for him and my name. I have never justified it and never will. Just as little as for the loneliness I felt back then on that bus—surrounded by all those people.

I began to read and explore the stories behind these injustices. Yet, over time, I realized that such divisions did not only exist in the past, nor were they limited to this bus. Discrimination has many faces. It does not only concern skin color or origin, but also gender, religion, social background, physical impairments, or other characteristics that seemingly divide people into categories and classify them. Some people's prejudices simply cannot be overcome, regardless of whether they concern skin color or the legacy of a great name. Some struggles, especially those for recognition and freedom, may never end.

I know nobody is perfect—and that includes me. I have probably made mistakes myself or unknowingly hurt people. But I want to keep an open mind, question myself, and learn from my mistakes. My father was always a role model for me in this respect. He showed me that it's not about elevating oneself above others, but about standing up for values that are crucial for respectful coexistence. I hope that I can continue on this path with the desire to help shape a world in which people are not marginalized because they are "different."

At the age of eleven, I was confronted with a truth that I had not known before, but which touched me deeply. These experiences sparked a desire in me to do my best to promote a society in which every person is treated with respect. Not because I feel I know better, but because I firmly believe that no one should be excluded or belittled because of what makes them special, but rather understood and accepted. I was in a new chapter in my life that challenged me for the first time in a way I never expected. Perhaps too early in my life, but definitely not too late.

My 15th birthday

Even as a teenager, it didn't get any easier. Situations where my boundaries were crossed kept happening, even on days that were supposed to be enjoyable. Like on my 15th birthday. I had invited a few close friends, as well as some acquaintances and classmates. It was a typical evening for a teenager—music, laughter, a little bit of freedom. But at some point, when the guests had broken off into small groups, something happened that I hadn't expected. One of the acquaintances I had invited suddenly pushed me into a corner. Without warning, he tried to kiss me. I didn't want that. I fought back. I tried to escape. But he didn't let go right away. It took a while before I could really free myself. I was shocked, not only by what had happened but also by how helpless I felt in that moment.

I told my mother. Two days later, this boy suddenly showed up at our door again in his car. He wanted to take me somewhere. I immediately told my mother, "I'm not going with him. You know what happened." Her response was, "Oh, it was just a silly boyish prank." But it wasn't. It was invasive. It was disrespectful. And it was wrong. I didn't go with him. Thankfully. Even though I may not have been able to put into words exactly what I was feeling at the time, I clearly felt that my "no" had to matter, even if others wanted to downplay it.

Assault in Italy—an alleyway on Lake Como

Unfortunately, assaults have been a recurring part of my life. Over the years, I counted five stalkers—and that was only the beginning. One of the worst incidents occurred in Italy on Lake Como. I was there on vacation with a friend. That afternoon, around 12:30 p.m., I was strolling alone through a small town market. The sun was high; it was warm and lively, and yet something felt different. Something was wrong.

As I left the market, I noticed a young man was following me. He only spoke Italian, but his stare made his intentions clear. I told him plainly—as clearly as possible with my limited language skills—to leave me alone. But he didn't. I got louder, more assertive, but he just grinned and came closer. Then everything happened quickly. Suddenly, I felt his arms from behind—hard, firm, and intrusive. He pressed himself against me. I tried to fight back, but he was stronger. With brute force, he threw me against a wall. My right upper arm scraped along the rough surface; the skin tore open and burned like fire. I gasped for breath, but he pulled me further. Away from the street. Away from the people. Deeper into a narrow, winding alley, toward a house with an open door. He wanted to drag me inside. He had a firm grip on my arms, and I could hardly move. I was trapped in the middle of this strange, quiet alley. Everything seemed to stand still.

But then something happened. My car keys slipped out of my hand and fell to the ground, the metallic clink echoing between the walls. For a tiny moment, his grip loosened. It was my chance. I took a deep breath, rammed my elbow into his stomach with all my strength, broke free, and ran without looking back. Just away. I could still hear him calling. He apologized, shouted after me to come back. But I ran. I ran as if my life depended on it—maybe it did. Only when I reached the main street did I dare to look back. I couldn't see him anymore. My legs were shaking. My whole body was tense, full of fear, full of disgust. I made it back to the hotel, locked the door behind me, and immediately jumped in the shower. I stood there for a long time, the water pelting my skin. But the feeling of filth, assault, and powerlessness couldn't be washed away. It was inside me. And it still is today.

The stalker from Landstuhl

Stalkers have been a presence throughout my life. One of the worst instances, however, occurred when I was living in Landstuhl and tutoring at a local study group. I taught there regularly, mainly German, while a man responsible for mathematics worked at the same institution. From the start, he struck me as odd. There was something unsettling about him, something hard to pinpoint, but definitely noticeable. The longer I worked there, the more inappropriate his behavior became. Initially, it was just verbal—intrusive compliments and unsettling comments. But it quickly escalated. Physical advances followed, touching that was clearly unwelcome. It wasn't severe enough to warrant immediate legal action, but it was far beyond acceptable boundaries. All of it simply made me deeply uncomfortable.

Then came the moment that changed everything: a handwritten letter. Among other things, it read: "I will kill you. I am the Prince of Darkness. We will die together." The rest continued in the same vein—threatening, deranged, and unpredictable. From then on, the situation spiraled out of control. He stood outside my window almost every night as soon as it got dark. He called me, both on my cell phone and on my landline. I felt unsafe everywhere. Escape was nearly impossible because he knew my car and where I parked it. He was often standing right there when I wanted to leave the house. It was like a never-ending nightmare.

I informed my parents, and together we went to the police. The response was sobering: "As long as there is no physical assault or rape, there is nothing we can do." We were stunned. Nevertheless, my parents hired a lawyer, and after that, the police at least drove past my apartment irregularly.

But he didn't stop. He knew where I was, no matter the time. He would suddenly show up in places where I had felt safe. He stalked me until the day he suddenly appeared inside my apartment. Thank God I wasn't alone; a friend was with me. We were able to run out together immediately—quick, instinctive, and without thinking. It's difficult to say what would have happened if I had been alone at that moment. Eventually, it stopped. Perhaps the police presence finally had an effect. Maybe there was another reason. I still don't know. But this experience remains one of the worst of my life.

The tampered vehicle

In 2005, during my legal clerkship in Landstuhl, I experienced a series of disturbing incidents involving my vehicle. I commuted daily to Nackenheim, near Mainz, which meant long drives in the early morning, often while it was still dark. I parked my car in a lot above my apartment. It was still dark when I went to get in. On the motorway, I suddenly noticed that something was wrong with my headlights. When I pulled over, I realized they had been smashed. I had them repaired and hoped it was nothing serious, as similar incidents had happened to me several times before. A few days later, my brakes weren't working properly. After an inspection by the towing service, it turned out that the brake lines had been cut. Although there was no direct evidence, and the car also showed signs of older wear and tear, the previous incidents reinforced my suspicion of deliberate tampering.

After the tampering with the brake lines, which could have caused a serious car accident, I should have immediately called the police. Repeated damage to vehicles is a serious criminal offense that can have significant legal consequences. If such acts are suspected, it is crucial to inform the police right away, even without concrete evidence at first. Other drivers could also have been involved on the highway. Although I knew I should have notified the police, I hesitated due to a lack of evidence. I decided to wait and see, which later turned out to be one of the biggest mistakes of my life. Thank God, I was lucky.

One morning, I discovered that my window had been smashed with a huge rock, and the leather seats had been slashed from top to bottom, with the filling removed. That was, of course, the moment I had to call the police. The police officer arrived immediately. They took fingerprints and checked everything that needed to be checked. Finally, he said something very frightening: "It would be better if you moved away from here. Otherwise, the perpetrator will do to you what he did to your leather seats." Despite the police investigation, I never found out who was behind these crimes or whether there were multiple perpetrators. However, I followed the detective's advice and moved away, which was probably a wise choice.

The story of the hit-and-run

I still remember the day the phone rang in my apartment in Landstuhl. It was an ordinary day when the police called to inform me that I had been reported for a hit-and-run. Allegedly, I had run a red light, hit someone, and then just driven away. The police explained that they had a witness who had described me, my car, and my license plate in detail. It was a moment that completely threw me off balance.

The police asked me to come to the station immediately to provide an explanation. It was difficult to process. I knew with absolute certainty that I had not been at the scene of the accident at that time, and I could prove it. Witnesses and evidence could have easily confirmed that I was elsewhere on that day at that time. The strange thing was that I didn't even have to provide evidence or proof to support my statement. My simple explanation that I was performing my legal clerkship at the time was enough to clear up the case. No further questions were asked, no further evidence was required—my statement alone seemed sufficient.

However, I never found out whether the police had actually verified my statement. But why were my name, my car, and my license plate number mentioned? It was too specific, too targeted. The question of why I, of all people, was involved in this matter remained unanswered. Despite my explanation and the lack of connection to the incident, the police were never able to properly explain how the accusations came about. The case was simply dropped without the full background being clarified. No one could give me an explanation as to why I was the suspect.

It was a bitter lesson for me. How quickly can you find yourself in a situation where you are simply accused of something without having any influence over it? How difficult is it then to fight against these suspicions, especially when they seem so concrete and targeted? The whole story is an unsolved mystery to me, and despite all the potential evidence and witness statements, the uncertainty remained: What had really happened? And why me?

The story of the hit-and-run

I still remember the day the phone rang in my apartment in Landstuhl. It was an ordinary day when the police called to inform me that I had been reported for a hit-and-run. Allegedly, I had run a red light, hit someone, and then just driven away. The police explained that they had a witness who had described me, my car, and my license plate in detail. It was a moment that completely threw me off balance.

The police asked me to come to the station immediately to provide an explanation. It was difficult to process. I knew with absolute certainty that I had not been at the scene of the accident at that time, and I could prove it. Witnesses and evidence could have easily confirmed that I was elsewhere on that day at that time. The strange thing was that I didn't even have to provide evidence or proof to support my statement. My simple explanation that I was performing my legal clerkship at the time was enough to clear up the case. No further questions were asked, no further evidence was required—my statement alone seemed sufficient.

However, I never found out whether the police had actually verified my statement. But why were my name, my car, and my license plate number mentioned? It was too specific, too targeted. The question of why I, of all people, was involved in this matter remained unanswered. Despite my explanation and the lack of connection to the incident, the police were never able to properly explain how the accusations came about. The case was simply dropped without the full background being clarified. No one could give me an explanation as to why I was the suspect.

It was a bitter lesson for me. How quickly can you find yourself in a situation where you are simply accused of something without having any influence over it? How difficult is it then to fight against these suspicions, especially when they seem so concrete and targeted? The whole story is an unsolved mystery to me, and despite all the potential evidence and witness statements, the uncertainty remained: What had really happened? And why me?

Got away with it

During my studies in Saarbrücken, I had many unforgettable experiences. The university was just outside the city, but we students often spent a lot of time together. One day, we took a trip downtown. As we crossed the streets, we were, of course, careful. We looked left and right, checked for oncoming traffic, and when we were sure the road was clear,

I took the first step. But just then, a car came racing toward me at high speed. I couldn't get out of the way fast enough, and the car literally threw me into the air.

I landed on the hood and then rolled onto the street. Fortunately, the driver was able to brake in time, and there was no serious accident. It was a huge shock for all of us, and the people who stopped stared at us, which I always find personally uncomfortable. In moments like that, you feel completely exposed to their gaze. I quickly jumped up. The driver came over to me, I said everything was fine, and he got back in his car, and drove away. At the time, I thought he should have called the police, and maybe I should have done that too. But in that moment, I was in complete shock, though I wasn't really aware of it. What I definitely should not have done was just get in the car and drive home.

It was about a 45-minute drive, which I started without truly realizing what had happened. When I got home, I rang the doorbell and my mother opened the door. Without saying a word, I rushed straight to my room, but, as mothers often do, she immediately had a bad feeling and followed me. She asked what had happened, and when I explained everything to her, she reacted immediately. She took me to the doctor, who said I needed to go to the hospital for an X-ray.

At the hospital, the doctor quickly determined that although no ligaments were torn—which was very fortunate for me—the impact had left me with some painful wounds. Thank God I had very stretchy ligaments, which spared me a lot of pain in this situation. Despite the bruises and contusions, especially on my right side, I didn't let that stop me from going skiing just two weeks later, because as the saying goes, "Like father, like daughter." It was a moment that would stay with me for a long time, not only because of the shock, but also because, despite everything, I had learned not to let it get me down—just as my father had taught me.

Human Dignity is Inviolable

There are experiences in life that stick with you forever. Things that shape you and that you may never be able to fully understand. But I have decided to tell this story, because I do not want to keep silent. I want to be honest, and I want to encourage other women.

This was not the first time someone had attempted to use violence, but it was the first time in this particular setting. What happened didn't align with how I saw the world. There was a man, a high-ranking politician, who held an office that was supported by the trust of the people. Someone I knew through my father, someone I trusted. But that trust, that sense of security I associated with him, vanished that day, giving way to feelings of helplessness and anger, but also strength and power. I'm not going to share that man's name, and that's not because I want to protect him or hide the truth. This is not about getting satisfaction or making headlines. I'm not the only one. There are so many women, girls, who could have told this story, who also experienced this kind of assault. What happened to me is not an isolated case, and that is the sad truth.

But today, I want to raise my voice to show that even I, who grew up in a seemingly safe environment—protected by my name, public image, and celebrity status—have had these dark things happen to me. And to strengthen all those who have never dared to speak out.

It was at one of those events we all know, with politicians, with people who have a lot to say. I had already met the man through my father and trusted him. That day, I thought nothing of it when he asked me if he should show me around the premises. I thought it was a nice, friendly gesture. But what happened next would remain etched in my memory forever. We came into his office, a large room that exuded responsibility and authority. We had a short conversation, a few trivial words. But then he turned to the door and locked it.

At that moment, when he approached me, I realized he was going to assault me. I had to defend myself. I acted purely instinctively, intuitively. I wasn't afraid; I suddenly had no respect for him, because in that moment, he was just a little man to me who had lost all right to respect. I had no plan. No idea what was right or wrong. I was still young, full of fears and doubts. But one thing I knew: I could not remain silent. So I stood up to him, told him in no uncertain terms that I would not remain silent, that I had a name, that my family was strong, and that I was prepared to go to the highest court if he harmed me.

I believe that at that moment he realized that, despite my young age, I was prepared to fight with everything I had and that I would not give up until I had obtained justice. I believe that this strength and the knowledge of my connections, of having a famous name behind me, made him back down. In the end he did not physically assault me, but what happened at that moment was not only about assault on my body, but also on my soul, on my trust in people in positions of power. But I would also like to emphasize that assault is not only committed by people in positions of power. It also happens in everyday life, in reality, by those who do not hold high offices.

Assault can happen anywhere, and it affects people from all walks of life. Not everyone in a position of power takes advantage of it like that. Many act responsibly and with respect for others. There are good and bad people everywhere, and it is important to keep reminding ourselves of that. I have never lost my faith in the goodness of people. I never lost that belief in goodness. There were many struggles, times when people tried to break me, but no one succeeded. I know that this is also thanks to my strong and loving parents, who always supported me and gave me strength. They showed me how important it is to never give up and always believe in myself.

But I can also understand those women or even men who, when something like this happens to them, do not speak up. It is an incredibly difficult step to take a stand and speak the truth. People feel ashamed and perhaps even inferior. Above all, they despise the person who did this to them. More than anything, however, there is the fear of not being believed and the fear of the long road ahead. I understand these fears, because telling the truth is not easy. But I can tell you this: You are not alone. There is always a way to fight, whether through your own silence or by finding allies.

I'm not telling this story to accuse anyone, but to empower, to say to all the women and men out there: "You are not alone." Because the worst thing that can happen to you is the feeling of having no power, the feeling of not being able to defend yourself. But I can tell you this: Defend yourselves! Be strong! Believe in yourself and in justice. You have a voice, and it matters. It is time for us to support each other. And above all, it is time for us to stand up and fight for our rights and our dignity—and that applies to all areas of life and to all people.

The experience in Turkey

Two years ago, I had another incident of this kind, this time on vacation at a five-star hotel in Turkey. I wanted to treat myself to a massage to relax, as I had severe neck and shoulder pain. The masseur led me into a secluded room. The massage itself went without any major issues, but when I said goodbye, he suddenly pulled me into an embrace and tried to kiss me on both cheeks. I found this inappropriate and told him so. But he didn't seem to care. After this first massage, I had an uncomfortable gut feeling, but I pushed it aside. I thought maybe I had become oversensitive because of the many incidents in my life. I didn't listen to my inner warning system—a mistake that would later have serious consequences.

The next day, I had my second massage appointment, again with him, and again in that remote room. But this time, the massage was different from the start. At first, he made me feel safe until I could no longer escape. He grabbed me with unnecessary force and applied so much painful pressure. Meanwhile, he kept repeating how good-looking I was and that he would like to get to know me better. I tried to move, to get away from him, but he held me tight. Then he said something that made me freeze: since I hadn't responded to his advances the day before, he would show me who was in control today.

What followed were 45 minutes of pain and helplessness. My whole body ached, and later I discovered bruises all over. Every attempt to free myself failed. Finally, he tried to kiss me and forced his tongue into my mouth. Only when I fought back with all my strength and screamed did he let go. I ran out of the room—shocked, disgusted, and unsure of what to do. I struggled with myself all day. I couldn't think straight and didn't know if I should report it. Even at night, I couldn't get this incident out of my head. I wondered if it was my fault, if I was to blame for it happening to me again, if I had just been lucky that it had only been assaults in the past.

But the next morning, I made my decision: I would inform the hotel management. No one else should have to go through what I had gone through. No one should have to suffer like that. So I went to the hotel manager's office and told him everything. The conversation was unpleasant and stressful. The management consisted only of men; a woman was only called in later. I had to tell my story several times and show my bruises and the marks left by his fingers. It felt degrading. I don't know if the masseur ever faced any consequences. The hotel management promised to take care of it, but he had already left the hotel. Apparently, it had been his last day of work anyway.

In The Spotlight: A Blessing And A Curse

I grew up in a gilded cage. On the outside, it glittered: immaculate and sparkling, the picture of a perfect life. That's how the world saw it: the daughter of a legend, the daughter of a hero. But inside, this cage was cramped, silent, and cold. I learned early on that my freedom was merely an illusion. I had to smile even when I didn't feel like it. I had to keep my tears to myself. I always had to put on the "right face," especially when the public was watching.

My mother made it clear to me, even as a child, that my job was to keep the family together. "You are the air I breathe, my calming influence," she often said. But with that attitude, she ensured I could barely breathe myself. It wasn't a tender declaration of love; it was an obligation. I was supposed to fulfill her expectations, live the dreams she never allowed herself to have. I was supposed to be strong, flawless, always conforming. Everything had to look perfect on the outside, even if it was crumbling on the inside. The mask could never slip.

And I played the part. I took a back seat, letting others shine while I smiled, nodded, and said "yes." I put on masks, changing them depending on the occasion and the audience. I learned to suppress my own needs until I no longer knew who I really was. I became a master of role-playing—always agreeable, always careful that no one spoke ill of us. The more I conformed, the more I lost the person behind the mask.

My father was different. He was above expectations, above people's gossip. I always admired his calmness and composure. And yet, he knew that one day I would carry on his legacy. In the last years before his death, he took me with him, showed me how to behave in public, how to maintain composure, and how to speak when everyone was listening. He knew I was the only one who truly understood and embodied soccer—the "Miracle of Bern." He knew I would be the one to carry it on, with pride, with respect, but also with the weight that came with it.

Yes, my life has often been difficult. There were times when I thought I would break under the weight of expectations, responsibility, and pain. But there was also light. There were friendships that remained, even in the darkest hours. I think of Nicole, who has been by my side for half my life. We experienced ups and downs together, walked through the rain, laughed, cried, and always found the sun again.

My life wasn't just duty, not just a cage. There was real joy, real laughter, moments that shaped me. Now I sit here and write. I feel my shoulders relax, I take a deep breath. I spread my wings—finally. No longer clipped. No longer in the shadow of expectations. I am ready to fly. For myself. For my parents. For my father. For my mother. For all the stories I will tell. And most of all, for what I am: a person who has learned to look ahead.

When a name becomes a burden

Journalists repeatedly asked me whether the name Eckel was more of a blessing or a curse. Although I had often considered this, I could never give a clear answer. There were simply too many times and situations in my life when the name Eckel actually felt like a burden—but really only because many people had certain expectations upon hearing it. I am proud of my name, but not because it is the name of a famous man. Of course, the name Eckel almost always elicits a reaction, even today, seventy years after the event that made it famous. The reactions are completely different. When I mention my name somewhere, someone who was initially reserved might suddenly ask in a friendly manner, "Eckel? Oh, do you have anything to do with the 1954 World Cup winner?"

Where there is light, there is also shadow

However, I also sometimes face sudden and clear rejection. People probably think I believe I'm special and expect preferential treatment. No matter where I go, as soon as people hear the name Eckel and know who I am, their behavior changes—sometimes subtly, but other times quite noticeably. It might manifest as people addressing me by name more often than necessary or mentioning something they know about my father. But it can also happen that people suddenly become reserved, often even dismissive. This usually occurs immediately.

It was already like that when I was in school. Even back then, my sister and I were often the center of attention, even though neither of us ever wanted it. As much as I loved the glamorous side of being at my famous father's side, I was also very aware of the downsides that come with a well-known name. This realization only developed over time. As a child, I often felt helpless in such moments. It was particularly painful for me that teachers, of all people, sometimes made snide comments—comments that hurt me deeply and that I still remember today.

I think it was in seventh grade in secondary school. Our teacher held a little class quiz, asking general knowledge questions. At one point, one of the questions was which soccer player was commonly known as "the greyhound." I honestly didn't know the answer at the time. But some of my classmates looked at me and shouted, "Come on, Dagmar, you have to know that. It's your father!" Only then did I recall having heard the term "greyhound" used in connection with my father before. I'm sure I felt a little proud at that moment that many of my classmates knew my father, but I don't remember exactly how I felt.

However, I remember my homeroom teacher's reaction all the more clearly. He said, "Yes, Dagmar, but you don't need to be proud of that. He's just a soccer player. What do you want with a father like that? All he can do is run after a ball." I was speechless. My face grew hot, my cheeks burned. I felt the stares of my classmates as they looked at me and grinned. None of them stood up for me. I felt completely alone.

Our teacher was about thirty years old, maybe a little older. Apparently, he knew nothing about my father except that he was called "the greyhound." He probably didn't even know that my father was a teacher himself. I didn't understand his words and couldn't respond. I considered teachers to be people deserving of respect. That's what I had been taught. And so I just had to endure this and similar humiliations. Statements such as that my father was just "a stupid soccer player" who could do nothing but run after the ball hurt me deeply. What was even worse was that this contempt was also transferred to me. Another teacher said to me in the schoolyard in front of other children that I was so stupid that I wouldn't even be able to work in a factory later in life. Such statements destroyed my self-confidence. When you hear that over and over again as a child, you eventually believe it yourself.

At this secondary school, it all started on the first day of school. The class teacher asked me if I was Protestant or Catholic. Our family is Protestant, but I wasn't familiar with the word Protestant at the time. Somewhat flustered, I reflexively replied that I was Catholic. When I later realized that Protestant actually meant Evangelical, I raised my hand to correct my mistake. But instead of understanding, the teacher showed only incomprehension, shook her head, and said, "How can you be so stupid and not know whether you're Catholic or Protestant?"

I didn't feel comfortable at this school from the very beginning, and that feeling continued throughout the following years. In elementary school, I was one of the best in my class. But in secondary school, my grades got worse and worse. At some point, I even started skipping school—sometimes for days at a time. I left the house in the morning as usual, but then hung around somewhere and killed time. Of course, this had a serious impact on my school performance. Eventually, I failed and had to repeat ninth grade. My parents didn't believe how much I was suffering from the situation. Nevertheless, I was determined to get my secondary school diploma. I knew I could do it.

It was only when I was about to fail a second time and my mother had met one of the teachers in question that my parents agreed to let me change schools. After tenth grade, I was allowed to transfer to the Heinrich Heine Gymnasium in Kaiserslautern. Before that, there had been a teachers' conference to decide whether I would be allowed to repeat tenth grade at all. When I arrived in my class that morning, some of my classmates greeted me reproachfully: "It's only because of you that this meeting is taking place today." Once again, I felt abandoned; no one stood up for me.

How changing schools worked wonders

Looking back, it seems almost grotesque to me that the principal of my old school opposed my transfer—not for educational reasons, but because of my name. "You see, Mrs. Eckel," he told my mother, "the name Eckel attracts students." I found it even more absurd that the teacher who treated me most disrespectfully during my time there described me as his favorite student years later. In any case, transferring to Heinrich Heine High School was a good decision. I was proud that my grades improved significantly there and that I was soon back among the top students in my class.

I never understood why I was subjected to such hostility. Perhaps teachers mentioned in conversations with colleagues or in the staff room that I was Horst Eckel's daughter. Whenever I mentioned my name somewhere, I was often asked if I was related to the soccer world champion. Perhaps that was precisely why some teachers wanted to show me that they didn't think my name was anything special and treated me accordingly.

But for me, Horst Eckel was first and foremost my dad. The fact that he was once a world champion hardly played a role in my everyday life. He was a modest and popular man, and no one had any reason to attack him. Perhaps it was precisely because of this general popularity that some people were jealous. And because they couldn't find anything to attack my father for, they directed their rejection toward me. I don't know for sure if that was really the case, but I can't find any other explanation for many of the things that happened to me. These are experiences I could have done without. I was also the target of ridicule and insults on social media on several occasions. I found it particularly cowardly when people hid behind anonymity. I would have preferred someone to tell me their honest opinion directly to my face. I could have dealt with that and perhaps cleared up any misunderstandings.

As a child and teenager, I was often helplessly exposed to such animosity. It made me feel deeply insecure. It was only as an adult that I learned to deal with such behavior better. After much reflection, I came to the conclusion that such attacks say more about the attackers than about me. But as a child and teenager, it often took me a long time to process those experiences. Fortunately, much of it fades with time. The details eventually disappear.

Between two worlds

I always felt like I was between two worlds. On the one hand, there was the world of celebrity, which I occasionally entered, much like any other ordinary person might step out of their everyday life and into the spotlight for an evening on certain occasions. On the other hand, there was the normal, middle-class world where my family was rooted, a world that we were also repeatedly thrust out of and into the public eye. I must admit that I always enjoyed this very much.

The galas and red carpets were fascinating to me, and I'm very happy that I was able to share those special moments with my family, especially my father. I thoroughly enjoyed those occasions, and I openly admit that I liked being the center of attention. But strictly speaking, I often felt like I was at the intersection of these two worlds and didn't truly belong to either. Being the center of attention also means being exposed to the scrutiny of others. This is true in beautiful moments, but also in unpleasant situations. Those who stand in the spotlight are not only the center of attention but also, in a way, in the pillory. The gaze doesn't just judge the exterior; it often pierces the soul. At least, that's how it often felt to me, and even today, little has changed in that regard.

I always felt uncomfortable when a supervisor introduced me to my future colleagues on my first day at a new job as the daughter of World Cup champion Horst Eckel. This sometimes led to colleagues initially viewing me with suspicion, probably because they assumed I would be conceited because of my name. But that was never the case. The Eckel name became famous through my father, solely through his achievements and accomplishments. I was always aware of that.

Unfortunately, my own achievements were often only seen in connection with those of my father and therefore were usually not evaluated objectively. It was already like that in secondary school. If I got a good grade, it was not uncommon for my classmates to tell me that my work was only graded so well because of my name. Good work was almost never recognized as my own achievement, but poor work always was.

Without exaggeration, such incidents were more of a curse than a blessing and led me to develop an unhealthy distrust of other people over time. That's why it was always difficult for me to find real friends. I have only one true friend, Nicole, whom I have been friends with for over thirty years. She has never disappointed me, and to her, I was always simply Dagmar, not the daughter of Horst Eckel, the world champion. Of course, I was also in one clique or another and had a certain circle of friends, but I hardly had any real, true friendships.

When it came to relationships, I was what you might call a late bloomer. Of course, I had a few boyfriends as a teenager and young woman. But despite all the infatuation, I still found it difficult to completely shake off my mistrust, which had basically become part of my nature. And I felt vindicated more than once. As everyone can imagine, it's not very flattering for a young girl or woman to be given the impression that people were less interested in me than in my name, because I felt that I was sometimes asked too often for my father's autograph or for a soccer ball with his signature. Hearing that a boy was dating Horst Eckel's daughter and not just Dagmar Eckel triggered some pretty mixed feelings in me.

I felt exploited, as I did many other times in my life. This reinforced my general distrust even more. I was never sure whether people were interested in me or just my name, so I soon stopped trusting anyone. I was hardly able to defend myself against such behavior; I had never really learned how to do so, quite the contrary.

Just don't push yourself into the foreground

Even as a child, my mother taught me to be accommodating and never to put myself in the spotlight. "Never push yourself forward," she always insisted. "People shouldn't think we believe we're better than them. You mustn't do that to your father. Never forget that everything you do reflects on us, especially your dad." And to make sure I always remembered this, she often added: "Remember, God sees everything!"

I internalized my mother's words so deeply that, in far too many situations throughout my life, I instinctively asked myself whether I was doing the right thing or whether my behavior might displease my mother or hurt my father. Even as a child, I disciplined myself so much that I wouldn't give in to my craving for chocolate, just to see if my willpower was strong enough. To be clear, I wasn't forbidden from eating chocolate. I could have simply gone to the refrigerator to get a piece. But I forbade myself and wanted to see if I could do it—if my will was stronger than my desire for chocolate—because I thought that with a strong will, I could achieve anything and change a lot.

Until I was six, I was a happy, cheerful, and carefree child. In my childhood photos, you always see a little girl who was constantly laughing. At that time, I never felt restricted; I felt as free as one could feel in a carefree childhood. But already in my last year of kindergarten, demands for certain behaviors began. Slowly, very gradually, I was forced into more and more rules and couldn't understand why I had to do one thing and wasn't allowed to do another. My mother placed an invisible bubble over my sister and me, within which we had to behave as she thought was right, but outside of which we weren't allowed to be who we were or wanted to be.

Our family was financially well-off, even if we weren't exactly blessed with great wealth. Nevertheless, I sometimes felt like I was in the proverbial golden cage. I could only move within certain, very narrow boundaries and was exposed to the gaze of observers most of the time. "Just don't stand out, don't give anyone any reason to talk." Over time, I developed into a chameleon of sorts that could change color as needed to adapt to its surroundings. In the same way, I adapted to all external circumstances. I wore a mask that hid everything that was going on inside me from the outside world.

While my sister rebelled against these narrow boundaries, I tried to bridge the differences between the two worlds. I was docile so as not to cause my parents too much worry, and as a result, I always found myself caught in the middle. I was a very sheltered child. My parents, especially my mother, were always there for me. But I often felt too sheltered, I felt confined. As a result, I mostly withdrew and was often alone with my thoughts. I immersed myself in books or let my thoughts run free.

Why I liked Little House On The Prairie so much

The television series Little House On The Prairie particularly captured my imagination. Although the series primarily depicted the great hardships of an American settler family in the 19th century, it also showed me a loving family where everyone was supportive of one another. The parents in this series always had time for their children and were understanding and open about all their problems. I longed for that kind of ideal world and for that level of understanding for the inevitable problems children and adolescents face. When I got into a fight with a classmate, or was even beaten up—which happened more than once—and then told my mother about it at home, I usually only heard, "And what did you do to make the other person act that way? Isn't it your own fault?"

That was another side of my mother's personality. Instead of comforting me in such situations, she often offered only rational explanations, which didn't really help me at the time. The parents in Little House On The Prairie always reacted much more understandingly than my mother when one of their children came to them with a problem. I wanted that understanding and care so much that at times I wished I could have been part of that family.

What particularly touched me was the fact that in the series, the father always called his second-born daughter "three feet tall." My father had always called me that when I was very little—sometimes "Daggi," but mostly "three feet tall"—long before Little House On The Prairie was ever shown on German television. Not least, the thoughts triggered by the protagonist's experiences led me to a belief that helped me through many difficult situations and prevented my spirit from being too severely damaged.

"Don't contradict anyone, don't do anything that could get us into trouble"—those were my mother's words. So, I increasingly adopted the role of a defenseless person who never talked back. My mother didn't mean any harm, but she herself had never learned to stand up to injustice or to object when an objection was truly necessary. She had grown up with far too many restrictions and had to mature far too quickly during the years of war. She basically had no real childhood, almost only duties. She passed that on to me. She didn't know any better. Johann Wolfgang von Goethe's wise saying, "When children are small, give them roots; when they are grown, give them wings," did not apply to us. I don't think I ever had wings. Or if I did grow any, they were clipped early on.

My mother's attitude, which made her think that I was probably the cause of any problems I had with other people, became more and more ingrained, continued to grow, and even reached a point where I didn't tell my parents how an acquaintance of my father's verbally harassed me in the VIP room of the 1. FC Kaiserslautern. I was standing in a group with acquaintances of my father. He himself was not present. We talked about everyday things and soccer. I mentioned that I had moved out of my parents' house and had my own apartment in Landstuhl, thinking nothing of it, so I was particularly shocked by the intrusive behavior and statement of a good acquaintance of my father's: "Then take me upstairs and I'll show you how 'it' works."

At the time, I just smiled awkwardly and didn't say anything. And, of course, I kept the incident to myself. I didn't let on at home, but inside I was almost torn apart. Because of my obvious reserve, which was probably visible to everyone, many people around me thought they could get away with almost anything with me. Fortunately, I have now been able to almost completely shed this trait. I now know that I no longer have to put up with anything that could rob me of my peace of mind. If I had had this attitude at the age of twenty, I would probably have shown this man, who wanted to show me "how it's done," what it feels like to be slapped in the face.

Unfortunately, I have only been thinking this way for a few years. To be precise, since my father died. Only now do I no longer feel responsible for tarnishing his name when I don't tolerate something and consistently stand up for my point of view. I am gradually developing into a person who is at peace with her own nature. Only now, in my mid-fifties, am I slowly becoming my father's daughter and no longer just the daughter of the world champion. And someday, I hope, I will simply be Dagmar Eckel.

Reception in honor of Fritz Walter

One side effect of my father's prominence was his frequent public appearances. Well into his old age, he remained a welcome guest at a wide variety of social events. Especially in my younger years, I would eagerly anticipate these events for days. It was by no means guaranteed that I would be allowed to attend. I remember a big reception in October or November 1990. At the time, my parents explained that I couldn't come. I was twenty-two years old, and the reception was in honor of Fritz Walter, who had recently celebrated his 70th birthday. If Fritz Walter was a father figure to my father, then he was like an uncle to me. I had known him for as long as I could remember. And of all times, I wasn't allowed to go to his big reception.

No matter how much I begged and pleaded, it didn't help. At first, anyway. But a few hours before it started, my mother came into my room and said, "Come on, get dressed; we're taking you with us after all." That reception was an unforgettable experience for me, perhaps even more so than for Fritz Walter himself. A red carpet was rolled out for the guests—including me—to walk on. Soldiers of the Bundeswehr stood in formation on the right and left, and helicopters circled above the venue because the then-Chancellor Helmut Kohl was also present. For most people, however, Kohl was only the second most famous Palatinate after Fritz Walter. I enjoyed every aspect of this reception: the prominent guests, the flurry of flashbulbs from the press photographers, the special atmosphere, and, above all, the exclusivity of the event. Only a select group of people were invited, and I was allowed to be one of them.

On many other occasions, however, I was invited personally. It was a matter of course that I accompanied my parents or my father to various events. I was always aware that I was only able to attend such events thanks to my father's accomplishments and fame. But at some point, it became normal for me. When 1. FC Kaiserslautern won the DFB Cup in 1996, I was at the final in Berlin. Together with my parents, I celebrated the victory with the team. I even got to hold the cup when it was passed around. A few days earlier, my family had coincidentally met the team while celebrating my birthday at an Italian restaurant. Later that evening, the players formed a circle around me and sang me a birthday song. My father, however, kept a close eye on me. He knew only too well that celebrations with soccer players could sometimes get out of hand. He wanted to avoid any talk that might be to my disadvantage later on.

Less extravagant, but equally impressive, were the galas, such as the famous Sports Press Ball. There, every guest was made to feel like someone very special. You could feel it as soon as you arrived: the car door was opened for you, and you were greeted by name. When I wore a short dress, I was very careful to get out of the car in such a way that no one could see up my skirt. I knew that such images were particularly appealing to the paparazzi.

An experience: walking the red carpet

I enjoyed every step of my slow walk down the red carpet, while at the same time being extremely careful not to trip. When I heard press photographers and journalists call out my father's name, and shortly afterwards mine—"Hello Ms. Eckel..." or "Hello Dagmar, please look this way..."—to get a photo or a short statement, I felt the adrenaline rush through me. I just felt great in those moments. Yes, I got used to the flurry of camera flashes. And yes, I openly admit: I enjoyed these appearances. The attention I received could be intoxicating. While my father wanted to get this hustle and bustle over with as quickly as possible because he felt he could "do without all the fuss," I enjoyed it and let it wash over me. For me, these appearances had something magical about them. It was like entering another world—even though I knew full well that it wasn't real.

Nevertheless, I always remained myself in such situations. I answered all questions as I always did, only not in the Palatinate dialect, but in almost pure standard German. And I was careful about what I said. I didn't want to say anything imprudent that could make me or my parents look bad. I avoided using overly casual language and refrained from making lighthearted comments. I was always in control, despite my inner tension. As hectic and loud as it was outside on the red carpet, as soon as you entered the event building, it suddenly became quiet. Almost silent. The magic of the flurry of camera flashes would suddenly disappear. Conversations were now conducted in hushed tones, but the tension was palpable—the anticipation of the upcoming event was in the air. It was only here that real small talk took place, which was hardly possible outside.

The 2019 Sport BILD Award in Hamburg was an event that I particularly enjoy remembering. Several soccer players, including Robert Lewandowski and Arjen Robben, were honored for their achievements. Jürgen Klopp, 'Coach of the Year.' joined the event via video link from Liverpool. Günter Netzer, together with sports presenter Gerhard Delling, received the award for best TV commentators of all time. And my father—the only soccer world champion present that evening—was presented with the Sport BILD Award for his life's work. When he stepped onto the stage to a standing ovation, it was an almost magical moment for me. He accepted the award with impressive composure and spoke so clearly and confidently, as if he received such honors every week. It was already well after midnight, because the lifetime achievement award is traditionally presented at the end of the event as the highlight. “This award is for all my teammates who were there,” he said in a firm voice, moving everyone in the room. I was proud and grateful to be able to share this moment with him.

Over the years, I met many famous personalities at such events—especially athletes such as Franz Beckenbauer, Philipp Lahm, and Lothar Matthäus. All of them world champions, just like my father. But there were also actors, musicians, politicians, scientists, and people from other areas of public life.

One particularly memorable encounter was with Pierre Brice, who played Winnetou in the Karl May film adaptations of the 1960s—a hero of my childhood. Pierre Brice was charming, amiable, and impressed me with his natural friendliness.

Once, physicist and scientist Ulf Merbold, the first West German astronaut in space, was also expected to attend an event. I had always been fascinated by him and his achievements. Unfortunately, his visit was canceled at short notice because he was stuck in traffic. Time and again, I was amazed at how many people—even decades later—reacted immediately to the name Eckel. My father never had to introduce himself. Everyone seemed to know him. For him, it was completely normal for strangers to approach him and address him by name. Since I almost always accompanied him, I was also greeted, but I always had to introduce myself because my father always forgot to do so.

During the World Cup, our family was invited to the games at the Fritz Walter Stadium in Kaiserslautern. During a match between Saudi Arabia and Spain, I actually sat in the same row as King Juan Carlos of Spain—just two seats away. I was always aware that I only had my father’s prominence to thank for such encounters. As much as I enjoyed these experiences, I also knew that they would one day be over when my father was no longer among us.

In moments like these, I often thought back to a small incident: my father was once asked for an autograph, and then I was asked for one too. I was about fourteen years old. When I asked why he wanted one from me as well, the man laughed and said, “Because one day it might be worth just as much as your dad’s.” My father laughed too and said, “Yes, that’s quite possible.”

The Horst Eckel Foundation – More Than A Legacy

Dancers in colorful, Oriental costumes spun across the stage. Their pirouettes were accompanied by the rhythmic applause of the capacity crowd in the Baldenau Hall in Morbach, very close to where our family used to run their sports hotel. Even before the performance, a band had warmed up the audience with lively music, and two soccer freestylers amazed everyone with their incredible tricks. The skills of the two young men, who juggled soccer balls while standing, sitting, and even lying down—at times even in sync—would have impressed even highly paid professionals. A magician then baffled the crowd with never-before-seen tricks, and musical interludes lightened the mood between program segments. The inaugural Horst Eckel Gala in May 2019 offered a rich array of sports and artistic highlights. By the end of the evening, I knew that setting up a foundation in my father's name had been the right decision.

"Full Throttle Into The 50s" was the motto of the gala, and the action on stage was just as fast-paced. The announcement poster featured a photo of my father on a motor scooter, a '54 Goggo 200' from the Glas company in Nuremberg. Every player on the world championship team, including national coach Sepp Herberger, had been gifted this scooter at the time. The company was proud to present the world champions with the luxury version, which included an electric starter. Of course, they seized this opportunity to advertise—back then still called 'Reklame': "Eleven world champions have only one ball. But each has his own Goggo." This was proclaimed on a typical advertising poster of the era.

This poster alone drew the attention of the guests. Just as visitors were waiting outside the hall, a light drizzle began to fall. Someone shouted, "How fitting. Now we have real Fritz Walter weather. Just as ordered." Amidst much laughter, they walked across the red carpet—straight through a time travel tunnel into the 1950s. Large-format photos hung on the walls to the right and left, illustrating key stages in the life and sporting success of Horst Eckel. There were also many family photos on display: from our time in Morbach, when my sister and I were still very young, and later from Vogelbach. This set the mood for the evening, which was opened shortly afterward by Roger Lewentz. The former Minister of the Interior and Sport of Rhineland-Palatinate emphasized that "Horst Eckel was not only one of the heroes of Bern," but that "the Eckel family lived and worked here quite normally in everyday life."

Eugen Gehlendorf, one of the vice presidents of the German Football Association, explicitly praised the foundation. "Dear Horst, you are the beacon of this foundation," he called out to my father. "It is people like you who give soccer a face." He continued: "It is personalities like you who make an impression and change the world. You experienced this yourself in 1954, when people cheered you on everywhere during your return journey from Bern. We owe the high regard, in which soccer is held in Germany, to you players, who represented our country so excellently at that time."

In addition to the performances, my father was particularly pleased that so many players from the Kaiserslautern team that had won the German championship eleven years earlier were present. They all knew my father very well. Although two completely different generations of soccer players had come together here, they got along famously. The conversations with these players, who could easily have been his grandchildren, were among the highlights of the evening, which was dedicated to the Horst Eckel Foundation.

Through his profession as a teacher, my father knew how important education is for a person's future and for society as a whole. For him, education and sport were closely linked. He wanted to use the power of soccer to instill a love of learning and knowledge in young people. “We want to train not only the head, but also the mind,” was his motto for the foundation. Sports programs for older people were also close to his heart. “I would never have lived to this age without my sport,” he said with conviction. The foundation was not only a matter close to his heart, but also became his life’s work in his final years.

In legal and business matters, the Sepp Herberger Foundation administered and organizationally supported the Horst Eckel Foundation. I contributed the entire initial capital of 10,000 euros from my private assets. The German Football Association donated the same amount in recognition of my father’s achievements. In the years that followed, numerous events were held to raise money for the foundation. Particularly noteworthy is the so-called Lotto-Elf, a soccer team that plays for a good cause on behalf of Lotto Rhineland-Palatinate. Many former professional soccer players, national players, and celebrities from other fields laced up their cleats for this team. My father was also still involved at the age of almost eighty. This came as no surprise to anyone who knew him, especially since his ambition was unbroken. There was an unwritten rule in the Lotto Eleven: “Anyone can be substituted—except Horst Eckel.” Although the team was founded in 1999, when my father was already seventy-seven, he made over a hundred appearances. Later, he coached the Lotto Eleven.

A moving moment was the concert by the Mainz Court Singers, held shortly before Christmas 2018 in the Simultankirche St. Philippus und St. Jakobus in our hometown of Vogelbach. I organized this benefit concert with Lotto Rhineland-Palatinate to support our foundation. The Mainz Court Singers wanted to thank my father for his social commitment, and that evening, we collected 3,500 euros in donations.

Unfortunately, the coronavirus pandemic in 2020 and 2021 prevented us from holding any further events. My mother’s increasing need for care and the two accidents my father had at home also kept me very busy. Nevertheless, we planned a second gala for my father's 90th birthday on February 8, 2022, with the proceeds intended for the foundation. However, this event never took place because my father passed away about two months earlier. Instead, I had to focus on arranging his funeral and later sorting through his estate.

Six months later, in August, the gala was finally held at the Max Grundig Clinic in Bühlerhöhe in the Black Forest, where his birthday celebration was supposed to take place. There were no elaborate stage acts, but an appropriate program featuring many well-known personalities—mainly soccer players—and it was once again a great success. The Horst Eckel evening in Hayna in the Palatinate in February 2023 was also a deeply moving event. An exhibition was held there, displaying many of my father's personal belongings and awards. Several hundred visitors attended over the two days—some almost reverently—viewing the contents of the display cases and the recreated scenes, such as our replica living room with the original music chest, which was a gift for winning the World Cup.

The tremendous response to this exhibition and the numerous friends and companions of my father who attended both the 2022 gala and the 2023 Horst Eckel Day showed me how enduring the enthusiasm for the 1954 World Cup winners is and how highly my father was regarded. I never expected so many people to accept our invitation and continue to support the foundation. That is another reason why it is so important to me that the Horst Eckel Foundation continues to exist after my father's death. But in November 2023, it became clear that the foundation could no longer operate under the trusteeship of the DFB. I needed a new trustee, and quickly, as I only had three months left. There were several options, but it was important to me to find the right partner, not just any partner. I needed someone who fully identified with my father's values and the purpose of the foundation.

I finally found this partner in the Bürgerstiftung Pfalz, which took over the trusteeship on March 1, 2024. With this connection, the future of the foundation, which was so important to my father, is secure, and that gives me a sense of calm.

Today, I not only have the strength to volunteer for the foundation but also—as described in the auction section of this book—to represent the interests of my father and our family against many obstacles without feeling inadequate or wrong. I feel strong enough to offer help and support to others when they ask me for it.

I am aware that this is a task that will probably never end. Nevertheless, I am ready to accept it. Not only out of empathy but also out of gratitude for having been able to discover this strength within myself. The journey through my life is also a journey toward healing and hope. This path is open to anyone who is willing to walk it, and no one has to walk it alone.

Finally, I would like to thank all the people who supported me in this book project and those who showed me along the way how much they appreciated my father. My thanks also go to all the readers who took the time to read this book and perhaps felt inspired to delve deeper into my father's story.

As the daughter of a celebrity, I—like everyone else—have control over how I shape my life, despite all the obstacles and despite all the comforts. I decide whether to step into the spotlight or remain in the shadows. Learning from experience and setting out on the path to independence is a worthwhile goal, even if you only start doing so in the second half of your life.

Between Heaven And Earth

I was born on May 21, 1968—right on the cusp between spring and summer, Taurus and Gemini, earth and air. Even my zodiac sign couldn't quite decide. Some people say I'm still a Taurus, others insist I'm already a Gemini. I'm somewhere in between, then—and it's precisely this 'in-between' quality that has been a defining theme throughout my entire life.

I am a child of transition, born on a day that unites two forces: the deep, earthy stability of Taurus and the light, quick-witted agility of Gemini. Sometimes I had both feet firmly on the ground; other times, my head was in the clouds, or as my grandmother used to say, "You always have one foot in heaven." I grew up with a deep sense that there was "more"—more than what could be seen, touched, or logically explained. It was never strange to me that things exist between heaven and earth that can't be named. I didn't have to search for them—they were simply present.

This openness to the invisible was deeply rooted in my family. It wasn't a lesson or a dogma, but something that simply existed, especially among the women in my lineage. Each woman carried something within her in her own way: an intuition, an inner connection, a quiet knowing. No big performance, no loud confessions, but always palpable. Like a subtle stream flowing beneath the surface.

The fortune teller

This vague feeling, this subtle, barely tangible energy, began shortly before my birth. Even before I saw the light of day, something seemed to be set in motion. My mother was pregnant with me, but she wasn't showing yet. It was a perfectly ordinary day. She was out and about in Homburg, in a parking lot, ready to do some shopping, when suddenly a woman approached her. This woman had a clear, penetrating gaze, but at the same time, her eyes held something deep and moving. A kind of quiet seriousness, combined with something that couldn't quite be named but could certainly be felt. My mother later called it a spiritual presence. She said this woman had a strong aura, as if she knew more than was visible. The woman stopped in front of her, looked at her, and said, "You are pregnant. And you will have a girl. This child will always have luck in misfortune. She will go her own way, and she has a great task to fulfill. It will be a difficult and long road, but she will walk it."

My mother was frozen in place. She didn't know this woman. No one could have known at that point that she was expecting a child—it was far too early, and there were no visible signs. And yet, this stranger stood there with a certainty that left no room for doubt. My mother got goose bumps, she told me again and again. At that moment, she clearly felt that these words were more than just an intuition—they were a kind of message.

She believed in such things, as I would later do, too. This encounter stayed with her. And yet, as the pregnancy progressed, it faded into the background a little. The family thought I would be a boy anyway. Perhaps that was also a reason why they put the woman's words aside for a while. But the fortune teller was right. Every single word was true. It was as if she had predicted my life: the luck in misfortune, the detours, the searching, the destiny that I always felt, even if I couldn't recognize it right away. And the path she predicted was truly long and difficult. But I walked it. And I'm still walking it.

The night in the public park

I was about nineteen or twenty, visiting my father in Kaiserslautern once again. There was an event where I met a young man who was working for the German Football Association at the time. He seemed reliable, sincere, with a strong character. At least, that was the impression he made on me. He asked if I wanted to go for a drink with him after the event. I spoke to my father, and although he was usually rather cautious, he let me go that evening. The agreement was clear: just one drink, and then I would return to my father and he would take me home.

So we set off. Suddenly, we were standing at the public park—a place that had always given me a strange feeling. I had never liked being there and only walked through it when absolutely necessary. I didn't know why we were walking there, of all places. We were actually heading in a completely different direction. But he said we should take a walk first. It was summer; it was already dark, probably around ten-thirty or even later. There was no one else around. The park lay silent and black before us. The wind rustled softly through the trees, and I felt goosebumps run down my spine. Not because I was afraid of him, but something about the situation didn't feel right. It was too quiet, too empty, too heavy. As we stood among the trees, he suddenly stopped, looked at me, and asked, "Do you feel something? Is there anything here that moves you?"

I hesitated. I did feel uncomfortable, yes. But I just said, "No, why?" I didn't want him to think I was weird. I had no idea what was coming. He pointed to a tree next to us. His voice changed, becoming more serious, quieter, more urgent: "This tree is special. A girl was hug here more than a hundred years ago. She was killed. It has to do with my story—with my father, with the argument I had with him. I don't know if I was the victim or the perpetrator back then. It was a kind of witch hunt... not like in the Middle Ages, but similar.

At that moment, the ground was pulled out from under my feet. I was paralyzed. All I wanted to do was get away. I searched for the exit with my eyes, but my legs wouldn't move. It was like a nightmare where you want to run but can't. I stood there, in the dark public park, alone with a man who was talking loudly about murder, guilt, and rebirth. I no longer knew if I was safe.

Then he said something that shook me to my core: "You are a medium for me. I work with a child ethicist—she deals with phenomena of this kind. You are my instrument. Through you, I am supposed to find out where my path leads. So tell me: what do you feel?" I had no answer. I didn't feel any clear message, nothing I could have told him. Only that I was sure: he wasn't the murderer. I tried to tell him that. And I told him that I felt uncomfortable in the situation and wanted to leave. We left the public park. I was still in a trance.

Outside, under the streetlights, he continued talking. He said I was very special. And then he said something else—something that still haunts me to this day: "There will be great changes. A wave of people will come to Germany from Russia—descendants of those who once went there with the Tsarina. Many more waves will follow, and Germany will be flooded. Politics will change. The climate will change. There will be big storms. Tornadoes, even here in Germany. And you will always be caught between Africa and Europe, if only for skin color. You will be come a great politician. But you will be murdered on the steps of an important building. You and your partner, stabbed or shot. It will be an assassination."

Then he took me back to my father without saying a word, turned around and disappeared. I will never forget that night. Not his words, not his gaze, and not the chill that ran through me. The most eerie thing of all is that some of his predictions actually came true exactly as he said. Point by point. And even today, when I think back to that evening, I get goosebumps.

Encounters

The encounter in the public park was one of the most profound of my life. But it wasn't the only one. Over the years, there were many others—sometimes unexpected, sometimes almost casual—and yet they never felt random. It was mostly women, always women, who approached me without my knowing them. I was often out with others, in a group, laughing, seemingly full of life. But I was drawn out of it, not by force, but by a look, an intuition that led directly to me. "You're laughing," they would say, "but you're not happy. Your eyes show something completely different." It was as if they could see right through me, as if they could see what I was hiding behind my mask. My eyes were not ordinary eyes; they reflected my soul, an old soul, they said, a sad one. And yes, in a way, it was true. I had learned early on to pretend. Not out of dishonesty, but out of protection. I never truly showed how I was feeling, but these women saw it, time and again. And to this day, I don't know how often that happened.

There were many times when I was not only internally "between heaven and earth," but also in a very real sense. Accidents, illnesses, near-death experiences. And yet, fate always chose life. I am grateful for that. During one of these phases, I was in the hospital. I was seriously ill—a virus no one could properly identify, no clear diagnosis, no certainty. I was lying alone in the room, powerless, on the verge of collapse. Then a nurse came in. She actually just wanted to quickly grab a copy of the newspaper, Die Rheinpfalz. "May I borrow the newspaper?" she asked. I nodded. Of course.

But then she stopped. She looked at me, not the way a nurse looks at a patient. This was different. Then she quietly asked, "Do you believe in angels?" Everything inside me immediately tensed up. Now something is coming that I might not want to hear, I thought. She noticed this, smiled gently, and reassured me: "No, don't panic. I just wanted the newspaper, actually. But now that I see you, I know it's more than that."

Then she sat down on my bed. "There are angels on this earth. Believe in them. You have several guardian angels, at least three. And you will make it. But you also have to believe in your angels." She spoke calmly, without drama. "You will have encounters—again and again—because you are a special person. And you have a great purpose. Maybe you already know it. Not concretely, but inside, deep down. And step by step, you will encounter this task. You will recognize it. And you will help many people." Then she added, "You are a fighter. And you are not only fighting for yourself." Finally, she took the newspaper and left. I was left alone in bed with this sentence in my mind: "You are not only fighting for yourself." I think she was right.

The ultimate proof of love

The moment in my life that confirmed everything I had long felt inside was the death of my grandmother when I was twenty-six years old. She was more than just a beloved relative. She was my soulmate, my steady anchor, my storyteller, my role model. A woman full of kindness, full of life, full of strength. She had survived two world wars, the death of one of her sons in World War II, the constraints of the times, and the injustice of the old order. And yet—or perhaps because of this—she was full of love. She was intelligent and alert right to the end. The pastor and the teacher once came to my grandparents and said, "Your daughter should go to secondary school—not your son."

But the times did not allow it. The decision was made, as was customary then: the boy went, my mother did not. My grandmother never forgot that. And she taught me the importance of education, justice, attitude, and history. She told me early on about King Solomon, not as a fairy tale character, but as a guide to truth and justice.

Then that day came. She was ninety-three years old. Physically frail, yes, but mentally crystal clear. And she knew what was coming. When the ambulance picked her up, she said calmly to my mother, "I'm not coming back." My mother drove behind them. I followed in my own car. For weeks, I had had this uneasy feeling, a premonition I couldn't shake. The doctors said her heart was too weak, her kidneys were failing. They attached a urine bag and said, "If it fills up, there's hope. If not..."

My mother stayed with her all night. In the morning, on her way to the hospital, she called me: "It's coming to an end." When I arrived, my grandmother was not in a room, but in a waiting area because the hospital was overcrowded. Yet she stood out. The doctors asked at reception, "Who is this woman? So well-groomed, so clear-headed—she's not from the nursing home, is she?" And my mother said in a firm voice, "No. She was with us. She lives with us." We sat by her bed, hoping, praying, and remained silent.

Then water filled her lungs. Slowly and inexorably. She was given medication for the pain. And at some point, she just went quiet. Her body stopped breathing. The nurse and the doctor declared her dead. A candle was lit. I didn't want to let that happen. Not now. Not like this. I sat down by her bed, took her hand, leaned over her, and whispered: "Grandma, I love you. We need you." And at that moment—at that very moment—she breathed. A deep, audible breath. She was alive. My mother cried out. The nurse rushed in, the doctor came back. Then my mother said quietly but firmly, "Go. Let her go. She was already on her way."

I was held back from the bed. I was supposed to leave. But I couldn't comprehend it. How could anyone comprehend it? My grandmother had already gone. And she came back for me. Just for a moment. Just one breath. But that breath was everything. It was one of the most difficult experiences of my life, alongside the deaths of my mother and father. But it was also a gift. The ultimate proof of love.

She was on her way and came back one more time. For me. What, if not that, is love? Since that day, I no longer just believe. I know: there is more between heaven and earth.

I have felt it.

I saw it.

And I experienced it through her.

A great task awaits

I had actually planned to end this book with the chapter about my grandmother. That was the most profound moment of my life, and it could have stood on its own. But my heart tells me there's something else that belongs here—something that offers a full circle moment with my father.

I had this same vague, quiet, yet insistent feeling with him, one I already knew from my grandmother. It began almost a year before his death. I couldn't explain it, but I knew something was coming, and I wanted to understand.

At that time, I sought out a naturopath. She specialized in regression, but without hypnosis. I wanted to stay awake, stay present, and not lose control. She was very empathetic and clear. She tried to take me back, layer by layer, with respect. But at a certain point, my body said no. I felt it clearly: my soul didn't want to go back. Not now. Not this way. And so we stopped.

What remained was a glimpse—her glimpse—of the connection between my father and me. Later, she sent me a message. I had given her the date, place, and time of his birth. What she wrote touched me deeply. She said I had lived before—with him. He had been my father then, too. Even back then, he was a well-known figure with a strong connection to the people. I had been his child, a daughter. But I couldn't inherit his legacy because I was a girl.

However, we had promised each other to return in another life to fight together. And this time, she said, as a woman, I would have the chance. I thought a lot about this "fighting together." About my life, about the people I had met who kept telling me I had a mission—a great mission. To this day, I still don't truly know what it is. But maybe it's quite simple: to carry on the legacy. To pass on the stories.

Their stories.

My father was Horst Eckel, a 1954 World Cup champion. He was part of the team that beat the legendary Hungarian team—a victory no one thought possible. A miracle, many called it. And for me, it is. These men were more than athletes. They gave a devastated nation something back: hope, courage, and pride. They weren't loud heroes or show-offs. They were people who transcended their own limits for others. And perhaps that is precisely my task: not to forget. Not to let go, but to carry on and pass it on. Perhaps my 'fighting' isn't meant to be arguing loud, but celebrating quiet remembrance.

Perhaps the great task begins with storytelling.

Farewell And Departure

I'm sitting here in Vogelbach, in the house that has shaped my family for generations, just two days after my father's death. Winter weighs heavy on the countryside; the sky is gray, the light subdued. It is quiet, but it's not an empty silence. It is a silence full of memories. I hear them in the creaking of the floorboards under my feet, in the ticking of the old clock on the wall, in the rustling of the bare branches outside.

I lean back, close my eyes, and then he is here. My father. Not the man the world knows. Not the legend, but my dad, who once told me in one of those quiet, intimate moments how, as a little boy, he stood all alone on the square in Vogelbach, playing with an apple. "I kept flicking the apple up with my foot, and it kept falling down. But I kept trying. And eventually it stayed up. And I laughed, a genuine laugh that came from the bottom of my heart. Not because anyone was watching me, not because I wanted to win something—simply because I made it do that. Because it was fun." I can picture him clearly, this little boy flicking the apple up again and again until he finally succeeds. He laughs, bright and carefree. And in that laugh lies everything that made him who he was: joy, passion, perseverance.

Back then, he wasn't thinking about becoming a world champion, about going down in history as a hero. All that mattered to him was that moment. The apple bouncing up and down. The pure joy of the game.

I open my eyes and look out at the square in front of the window. The grass is frozen, hoarfrost covers the ground, and the bare trees cast their shadows. I imagine him still standing there, that little boy, playing simply for the love of it. I smile softly. I know he's here. That he sees what I'm doing. That he approves. We talked about it. And yet, I miss him. And

I miss my mother, too. Especially in moments like when I was sitting at the FCK's 125th-anniversary celebration on June 2, 2025. I sat there at the table, looking at the screen, watching the images that were being shown—pictures of him when he was young, as he grew older, right up until shortly before his death. And I could barely hold back the tears. I saw him there, saw him laughing, and it filled me with a mix of sadness, happiness, and melancholy. I saw everyone else around me, heard their words, and even though those words didn't ease the pain, I also felt joy that he won't be forgotten. That the whole team from back then won't be forgotten.

I was there to represent him. During a break, I went outside and sat in his seat in the north stand. How many years I sat there with him, how many happy years, how many sad years. The Betze is like a second home to me. And it was the same for my father. He didn't leave, even when he was offered a lot of money to do so. No, he stayed. He said, "If the others aren't leaving, why should I? It's my, my, my home club. I can only be grateful that I was allowed to play here."

Yes, that's how he was: modest, down-to-earth, and kind-hearted—sometimes perhaps even too good-natured. He was someone who had to stand up for himself from time to time or even bang his fist on the table. But when things really got too much for him, he could do that, too. I respected him greatly for that trait. I never heard him say a bad word about anyone else. And this is where it all comes full circle for me: back at his workplace, back on the field, where I could feel very close to him because soccer was what connected us.

There are pictures of him everywhere here, a statue outside, with his team, with Sepp Herberger's quote: "The role of the underdog is the key to a treasure trove of immeasurable strength which, when awakened and fueled, releases energy and helps move mountains."

Unforgettable—that's exactly what he was.

I spoke quietly to him, thanking him for the wonderful time we had together. And I know he hears me. I know my mother hears me, too. I believe in that. And that belief gives me the strength to carry on the legacy of my father, the last living soccer world champion from 1954, to keep it alive for future generations and to make him proud.

And quietly, almost whispering, as if he could hear me—he can hear me—I say: "You know, Dad, I'm proud of you. Not because you were a world champion. Not because you are a legend, but because you always remained the boy who simply enjoyed improving himself. Who never gave up. Who always cared about other people. Your modesty defined you, but so did your fighting spirit and your discipline."

I imagine him looking at me, nodding, with that mischievous, quiet smile he always had when he knew he had done something well. And I hear his voice saying softly:

"Well done, my darling."

www.ingramcontent.com/pod-product-compliance
Lightning Source LLC
LaVergne TN
LVHW010653110826
845149LV00014B/3070

* 9 7 8 3 9 8 2 7 7 9 3 3 1 *